MW00326240

"Stephen Finlan offers a lucid and thorough critique of the view that 'Christ died for our sins' is a central tenet of Christianity. He shows that neither Jesus himself, nor much of the New Testament, nor the Greek patristic tradition thought so. Sacrificial metaphors, used in diverse ways by the apostle Paul, had an afterlife in Christian theology, abetted by psychological and social needs. This will be a provocative and illuminating read for pastors and lay Christians alike."

—HAROLD W. ATTRIDGE
Yale Divinity School

"Passionately rejecting those aspects of traditional atonement theory that implicitly turn God into a severe, sacrifice-demanding Father, and instead, pointing out the biblical evidence that reveals the original teaching of Jesus as emphasizing a generous and merciful loving God, Stephen Finlan's remarkable slim volume, *Salvation Not Purchased*, must absolutely be read and reflected on by all who preach and presume to teach others how to preach the Christian doctrine of salvation."

—ROBERT J. DALY, SJ
Boston College

"By putting—and keeping—Jesus square at the center, Stephen Finlan gives us an extraordinarily helpful treatment of atonement theology. *Salvation Not Purchased* is concise and accessible, but also rich in detail and analytically strong. Finlan starts with the right question—what do we learn from Jesus's life and teaching about salvation?—and then shows how satisfaction atonement theology distorts the gospel. A book with strong ethical implications."

—TED GRIMSRUD
Eastern Mennonite University

"In this book, Stephen Finlan redeems the traditional theories of atonement and hell by ridding them of their manipulative 'bad news' gospel message that depends solely on the economic sacrifice of an innocent victim before God can or will forgive sin. Instead, by exploring the Bible in its original languages and contexts, Finlan offers readers a gospel message that is truly good news from beginning to end. He presents these significant and provocative ideas with a pastoral heart and extends to his readers practical suggestions for living out the good news for the glory of God and for the furtherance of the divine kingdom. *Salvation Not Purchased* is a beautifully written, accessible, practical, and theologically stimulating book, one that I plan on using with church groups and in my undergraduate college courses."

—SHARON BAKER PUTT
Messiah College

"In *Salvation Not Purchased*, Steve Finlan continues to popularize his insightful research on Pauline atonement metaphors, making it accessible to a broader audience of ordinary Christians. In fact, one does not need to agree with his interpretation of animal sacrifice, nor with his type of incarnational Christology or his use of the gospels, in order to appreciate his zeal to correct and present alternatives to an entirely unhealthy Christian theology of penal substitution. Finlan's small book is a biblical theology approach of sorts, a plea for a decent, biblically based, liberal theology of salvation through Christ, and an interesting reflection on the psychologically damaging consequences of a conservative atonement theology."

—THOMAS KAZEN
Stockholm School of Theology

"Stephen Finlan takes the reader through Scripture and into the early church fathers and even some modern psychology to put to rest the historical misunderstanding of the metaphor responsible for thinking that Jesus must die for the Father to forgive the sins of humanity. Blood and sacrifice are powerful metaphors for the Jewish audience, but Jesus is the healer, co-creator, and goal of Christian life who reveals in his person the unbounded healing mercy of God. This book is a treasure for pastors preaching as for anyone interested in sound exegesis to dispel misguided notions of atonement and sin that have prevailed too long in Christian communities."

—TERENCE MCGOLDRICK
Providence College

SALVATION NOT PURCHASED

SALVATION NOT PURCHASED

*Overcoming the Ransom Idea to Rediscover the
Original Gospel Teaching*

Stephen Finlan

CASCADE *Books* • Eugene, Oregon

SALVATION NOT PURCHASED
Overcoming the Ransom Idea to Rediscover the Original Gospel Teaching

Cascade Books
An Imprint of Wipf and Stock Publishers
199 W. 8th Ave., Suite 3
Eugene, OR 97401

www.wipfandstock.com

PAPERBACK ISBN: 978-1-7252-5582-1
HARDCOVER ISBN: 978-1-7252-5583-8
EBOOK ISBN: 978-1-7252-5584-5

Cataloguing-in-Publication data:

Names: Finlan, Stephen, author.

Title: Salvation not purchased : overcoming the ransom idea to rediscover the original gospel teaching / Stephen Finlan.

Description: Eugene, OR: Cascade Books, 2020 | Includes bibliographical references and index.

Identifiers: ISBN 978-1-7252-5582-1 (paperback) | ISBN 978-1-7252-5583-8 (hardcover) | ISBN 978-1-7252-5584-5 (ebook)

Subjects: LCSH: Atonement. | Jesus Christ—Crucifixion. | Salvation—Christianity.

Classification: BT751.3 .F50 2020 (paperback) | BT751.3 (ebook)

Manufactured in the U.S.A.   08/13/20

CONTENTS

PREFACE

As a pastor, I am concerned about the truly harmful effect that certain Christian beliefs are having on believers. Specifically in the area of atonement ("Jesus died for your sins"), there are some unhealthy, untrue, and unbiblical notions that are causing distress and confusion among Christians. It is my *pastoral* concern that drives me to speak up about these troubling beliefs.

One such idea is the notion that salvation was "purchased with blood," that we are saved only because Jesus bled and died for us. Now, this says something good about Jesus (that he died heroically for others), but it implies something horrible about God the Father who would *require* such a sacrificial "price" or "ransom." This would place a huge gulf between a stern Father and a merciful Son, which deeply contradicts the Bible. Many Christians need to face the fact that they have accepted the notion of a spiteful and violent God, an idea that goes against Jesus' own teachings. This concept teaches us to be afraid of God, uncertain about the afterlife, and judgmental toward others—in direct contrast to the spirit and the content of what Jesus taught.

Since this is a problem with *beliefs*—with ideas that some Christians have about God—I will investigate the development of these beliefs, but my real interest is spiritual. Belief is *mental*, having to do with concepts and doctrines held by the mind. Faith is *spiritual* and relational; it concerns one's spiritual health, one's relationship with God, and how one treats others. Since actual spiritual values and loyalties are more important than mental notions, it is fair to say that *faith* is deeper than *belief.*

But beliefs still matter! Unexamined beliefs can do damage to people's faith, leaving people confused about what God is like, and making it hard to trust God. As a result of distorted beliefs, sometimes even *conflicting* beliefs, many believers become discouraged, and some even lose their faith, or at least lose confidence *about* their faith. Furthermore, as mentioned, our faith-relationship with God has a deep effect on our relationships with people. If we believe that God is vengeful and cruel, we might allow ourselves to be vengeful as well, and use our beliefs to justify our nastiness. Violent God-concepts do real and lasting harm, psychologically and ethically. If we fail to recognize God as a loving parent, we will make many wrong assumptions about God.

And so, it is in order to help people's *faith* that I am willing to critique some widely accepted beliefs. If your faith is strong enough to allow you to delve into doctrine without feeling threatened, then this book is for you. If you want to remain safe in your assumptions without examining them, without holding them up to the light of what Jesus said, then this book is not for you. I am asking that we question some of the things that are commonly said about God, so that we may really "understand these things" (John 3:10).[1]

This is a plea to my fellow Christians for us to be thoughtful as well as heartfelt in our beliefs. It is really a plea for us to love God with all our *minds*, as well as with all our hearts and souls (Matt 22:37). If we love God will all our minds and hearts, we will be unafraid to examine a serious problem that has become lodged within Christian belief.

Let us dive in.

---

1. I am using the New Revised Standard Version (NRSV) for Bible quotes, except when otherwise indicated.

INTRODUCTION

GOD-TALK

Some Christians can be heard saying something like this: "That should have been *me* up there on the cross, instead of Jesus. He paid my penalty and purchased my salvation." This shows an intense gratitude for Jesus' heroic life and death. It shows both a reverence for Jesus, who was sinless, and an awareness of one's own sinfulness.

Unfortunately, the comment also implies a very troubling concept of God. It assumes that God demanded death as a payment for sin, but was fine with letting God's innocent Son suffer that death on behalf of others. It assumes the existence of some law that there *must* be vengeance, even if the guilty parties are not the ones who suffer the vengeance!

Think of what this actually says about God the Father! It means that all God cares about is that *somebody* suffer for sin, even if it is an innocent person. Why such a violent setting for salvation? The answer that is commonly given is that God was *unable* to offer salvation until someone "paid the price," which assumes that God *cannot forgive*, that God must obey some law that demands punishment (or else that God *created* such a law). It is also diminishes God to a transactional relationship in which salvation is bought through the suffering of another.

This is a terrifying choice. If God *could not* forgive sin until a sacrificial payment was made, then God would be subject to a law that is greater than God. That would make God weak. On the other hand, if God *would not* forgive sin until a human sacrifice was made, then God would be cruel, demanding a terrible retribution, but satisfied to have it directed against the one person who is truly innocent. This would not really be God, would it?—at least not the God of *Jesus'* teaching.

Have we been projecting our human, material ideas upon God, and then defending them without checking to see if they really fit with what Jesus himself taught? Remember what Jesus said about the Father, both in his sayings and in his stories (parables). Jesus taught that God both *wants* to forgive and save people, and is *able* to do so: "Do not be afraid, little flock, for it is your Father's good pleasure to *give* you the kingdom" (Luke 12:32). God is genuinely forgiving and inviting, and need not be persuaded. Salvation is God's own gift, freely given. The door is wide open, and God invites us in!

Salvation is the most important subject. Jesus was always extending salvation, revealing God's nature, and working to build the family of God on earth. What did he say about God's attitude toward us, and how we get saved?

THE OUTRAGEOUS GENEROSITY OF GOD

Consider the parable of the Prodigal Son. First we must know that the conventions of the time said that fathers had status and honor, and that sons were supposed to be respectful and obedient. In the parable, the first act of disrespect is when the younger son impatiently demands his inheritance. That is rude and selfish, but the father goes ahead and gives him his share of the property (Luke 15:12). The son takes it, goes off, and behaves badly, ending up in poverty, having to tend swine. What a shameful situation for a Jewish young man! He has an awakening and makes up his mind to return and beg forgiveness from his father. He carefully works on his apology speech, which will include a heavy dose of self-humiliation. He plans to say "I am no longer worthy to be called your son; treat me like one of your hired hands" (Luke 15:19).

He sets off for his father's home, and when he was still far off, "his father saw him and was filled with compassion; he ran and put his arms around him and kissed him" (15:20). He is delighted to welcome his long-lost son. The son starts to give his self-shaming speech, but the dad doesn't even want to hear it. He needs no apology, no humiliation, no admission of guilt! It seems that he interrupts the son, orders the servants to bring out the best robe, a ring, and sandals for the young man, and a fatted calf to be slaughtered for a feast (15:21–23).

The father whom Jesus pictures is shockingly forgiving. He is not at all concerned with his own image, reputation, authority, or even his honor. He *runs* to greet the son, and never asks for any expression of submission or shame. In fact, he showers honors upon him. Jesus knew how surprising this image of an astonishingly kind and forgiving father would be. Even today, it is more than many believers can accept. A father who would embrace his irresponsible son without shaming or scolding him is *still* very counter-intuitive for many people.

When the other son, the self-righteous one, refuses to join in the joyous celebration, the father says "we had to celebrate and rejoice, because this brother of yours was dead and has come to life" (15:32). In other words, "don't you get it? I am forgiving and loving. You need to forgive and share in the joy of your brother's return. Stop being so joyless and judgmental! I am not about assigning blame, inflicting punishment, or demanding submission."

This goes against the beliefs that many people have about God. Many assume that God must be authoritarian, demanding, and punishing. They take it for granted that *strength* must come with *violence*. But Jesus goes out of his way to shatter that idea, to show that God is energetically loving, and is strong enough to forgive, to heal relationships, and to change human lives. God embraces, gathers together (John 11:52), seeks out and saves the lost (Luke 19:10), does not set out to *punish*, but simply to *save*! God is love (1 John 4:16).

Jesus tries to get people to accept that God is extraordinarily kind and inviting, but this is too radical for many to accept. How can there be no payment system, no repentance schedule, no penance imposed upon either the prodigal son or upon us? And yet, Jesus shows that salvation is available to *anyone*—even to a bratty son—who sincerely turns to God.

Sincerity is the key. This story does not teach that it is all right to be lazy and irresponsible. The parable only works if we assume the young son is honest, and his repentance sincere. Dishonesty is spiritually fatal. There is no salvation for the insincere, the pretender who is trying to get cheap forgiveness for evil behavior, but will actually go on misbehaving. It is doubtful whether a habitual liar can be saved at all: "the liar will perish" (Prov 19:9). Jesus' message of mercy is not meant to remove the necessity of moral seriousness on our part. But it is helpful if this seriousness is *love*-motivated rather than *fear*-motivated. One does one's best for a beloved parent because of *love*, not from anxious fear of punishment. If we truly love God, we will not be lazy, but will exert every effort to follow God's way, seeking to embody God's spiritual values. To understand the parable, one must have some of the same honesty and sincerity that the young son has.

Sometimes it is hard for us to accept the unconditional kindness of God. It may go against what we have learned. But if we open our hearts sincerely and learn about God's love, then we can understand what is meant by this: salvation is God's gift, not paid for, but freely granted. Jesus gets this message across by showing the father in the story being so generous, and demanding no payment through penance or suffering. There is no retribution, no punishment, only restoration and rejoicing.

God's generous desire to save is also the point of the nearby parables of the Lost Sheep and the Lost Coin. "Which one of you, having a hundred sheep and losing one of them, does not leave the ninety-nine in the wilderness and go after the one that is lost until he finds it?" (Luke 15:4). Is Jesus saying the shepherd will neglect the ninety-nine? Of course not. He is using this exaggerated imagery to show that one "sheep" really matters, and the shepherd will go out and rescue that one! God cares for *each individual person*.

There is "joy in heaven" when the *one* is found and recovered (15:7).

Similarly, a woman who loses a coin will sweep the floor, light the house, and search until she finds it, for there is *value* in the one coin (15:8–10). There is *value* in the one human being. The three parables in Luke 15 show God *seeking* out the lost to save them, without any punishing, scolding, or making anybody "pay." The emphasis is on God's love and generosity.

Jesus went out of his way to try to convince people that the Father is loving, all wise, abundantly forgiving, and provides a way for us to grow Godward. But people always find it hard to accept new ideas without mingling them with some old and unexamined ideas that they are carrying around. This happened with the early Christians as well.

One of these old ideas (held by Gentiles as well as Jews) is that justice requires retribution. A recent book by Ted Grimsrud shows how Jesus rejected the common belief that wrongdoing *has* to be met with violent retribution. He argues that "the logic of retribution" is still "deeply ingrained in the religious consciousness" of many Americans who assume that "God's holiness or honor" has to be "satisfied" through some act of retribution against sin.[2] Grimsrud points out (as I will) that Jesus heals and saves people simply out of God's desire to make them whole, and without any accompanying theology of retribution. When he shows compassion to people, he is showing them *God's* compassion, but they are slow to learn, even the ruler of a synagogue, to whom Jesus says: "ought not this woman, a daughter of Abraham whom Satan bound for eighteen long years, be set free from this bondage on the sabbath day?" (Luke 13:16). He is trying to get the ruler to see that God cares so much more for this woman's real needs than for rigid Sabbath rules!

But people were constantly misunderstanding Jesus, especially his own apostles. Jesus had to scold James and John when they asked if they could call down fire upon Samaritan village, in retribution for their lack of welcome (Luke 9:52–55). He worked

2. Grimsrud, *Instead of Atonement*, 5, 7.

tirelessly to wean the apostles from their biases and misconceptions. How often do we allow our material and earthly concepts to diminish our understanding of God?

Let us look into this by digging more deeply into the biblical record. By the way, this does not imply that I consider the Gospels to be flawless records, like tape recordings, but I *do* consider them to be largely reliable reports.

ASSUMPTIONS ABOUT GOD

In upcoming chapters, I will address the genesis of the images of sacrificial atonement and ransom. For now, I can mention that our earliest source for the sacrificial and purchase metaphors for the death of Jesus is the Apostle Paul, who was writing in the 50s AD. Paul is also the source of that extremely unfortunate slogan: "you were bought with a price" (1 Cor 6:20; 7:23). Paul's successors took his metaphors quite literally, blending the notion of sacrifice with the image of ransom and coming up with the idea of the death of Jesus as a ransom payment for the sins of humanity, the idea called "atonement" in theological circles.

In this chapter, I want to respond to the idea of atonement that is popular *today*, by contrasting it with the teachings of Jesus. My argument is less with Paul than with his more literal-minded successors, and with the crude atonement ideas that developed over time. It is the *purchase* concept that is most problematic.

The main problem with teaching that Jesus' death paid for human sin is that it slanders the character of God the Father! If God was either *unable* or *unwilling* to forgive without a payment in blood, then God was either weak or cruel. Both are false. God was not compelled to demand that a payment for sin be made, nor was God defending God's honor. Such ideas emerge when people apply *human* laws and attitudes to God.

"Somebody had to pay" is based on a series of mistaken assumptions. One is that God is stern and demanding, while Jesus is merciful and kind. This goes against Jesus' own teachings about his *similarity* to the Father: "Just as the Father raises the dead and gives them life, so also the Son gives life ... Whoever has seen me has seen the Father" (John 5:21; 14:9). There is no spiritual contrast between the Father and the Son; they have the *same love*. This is the good news: there is a circuit of love that flows from the Father, through the Son, to the Spirit, into us, and then among us.

Of course, no Christian wants to say that God is either cruel or weak. Yet Christians commonly fall into that trap unawares, accepting formulas that Christian authorities have told them they *must* believe, usually accompanied with a fierce and angry energy. Most believers follow their leaders. Instead, we should reflect upon what we have been taught, and see if it needs to be questioned, in the light of Jesus' *own* focus on love and forgiveness. What did Jesus himself teach about salvation?

SALVATION NOW

Jesus made it clear, in his preaching and his ministry to people, that the kingdom of God has come; it is *here*. Jesus built people up spiritually and told them they were *already* saved by their exercise of faith. There are *seven times* in the Gospels where he tells people "your faith has saved you," even when he has performed a miraculous healing for them. I am counting the times the NRSV renders it "faith has made you well," as well as the times they translate the *same verb* as "has saved" (Matt 9:22; Mark 5:34; 10:52; Luke 7:50; 8:48; 17:19; 18:42). The verb is σώζω (*sōzō*), which has the *primary* meaning of "saved." In all seven passages, the verb occurs in the perfect tense (*sesōken*), so it actually means "has saved." The choices "made well" or "made whole" make sense in their context, but so does "saved," and I prefer to stay closer to the verb's primary meaning.

By no means am I arguing that people are self-saving. That would be too rigid a reading of "your faith has saved you." Rather,

Jesus is generously giving them credit for their faith, and their role in *receiving* salvation. Actually, salvation results from both the divine *downreach* and the human *upreach*: the coming together of God's love (embodied by Jesus) and a person's sincere and faithful plea. Jesus does do miracles of healing, but he likes to lift people up and include them. He acknowledges their *receptivity* to the act when he says "your faith has saved you." Jesus certainly is the Savior and the Healer, but he likes to emphasize the human end of the divine-human connection.

Throughout the Gospels, Jesus saves people, and *tells* them they are saved. Without any reference to his coming death, without any substitutionary (taking the place of others) doctrine, he makes it clear that people's faith has *already* saved them. Again, the way to salvation and eternal life is *wide open*. Salvation is made available here and now, whenever people "hear the word, hold it fast in an honest and good heart, and bear fruit with patient endurance" (Luke 8:15; see also 8:21; 11:28). Notice how crucial is the "honest and good heart"—the *sincerity* of the person. Anyone who honestly recognizes the *need* for salvation can receive it.

Jesus is the Savior, not because of his death, but because of his divine identity, his power as Creator. He is the one who gave us life in the first place: "Through him all things were made; without him nothing was made that has been made. In him was life, and that life was the light of all mankind" (John 1:3–4 NIV); "in him all things in heaven and on earth were created" (Col 1:16). Jesus is the Savior in *exactly the same way* that he is the Creator ("he also created the worlds," Heb 1:2). He was the life-giver in the beginning, and he is the *eternal* life-giver now.

Jesus extends salvation just as he extended healing. In fact, the main images for salvation in the Gospels are healing and restoration. His healings were a gift of life, or a restoration of healthy life, and salvation is the gift of *eternal* life. Jesus was the life giver before he ever came to earth in human form. There is no magic in the crucifixion; he did not become the Savior only after he was murdered. He was the Savior from the start. In fact: "In a sense, we were saved by Christ before he was born."[1]

Salvation and forgiveness truly are the free gifts of God, not something purchased with blood. The problem with the blood-purchase concept is not what it says about Jesus, but what it says about God. It pictures God as harshly judgmental, and also corrupt: needing a victim, but willing to be satisfied with an *innocent* victim. What good is it to see Jesus as kind and good, if we see God as sadistic, corrupt, or weak?

There is something not quite healthy in the obsession with blood, as seen in Billy Graham, for instance: "Blood redeems . . . Blood cleanses . . . His blood pumps through your spiritual veins with eternal life . . . Blood justifies . . . Jesus paid for our sins with His blood."[2] William Placher wrote "Christ is our sacrifice. His blood transforms us into people who can once again come into the presence of the holy God."[3] This seems like blood-magic. Further, isn't it an over-emphasis on Jesus' death? Shouldn't we be focusing upon his *whole* life, his experience of God, and what he actually taught?

The teachings of Jesus go right against the notion that there would be no salvation until he had spilled his blood. God does not need to be paid or *persuaded*. Rather, God *already* loves us: "The Father himself loves you" (John 16:27). God's loving attitude is no different from Jesus' loving attitude. "Whoever has seen me has seen the Father" (John 14:9). If we recognize the character and the love of Jesus, we should recognize that these are also the character and love of God. No Christian who understands that will ever again think that the Father required the crucifixion of Jesus—or of anyone.

We should stop assuming that God needs *any* transaction, *any* payment. God's arms are wide open to receive. God is loving, like *any* good father: "Is there anyone among you who, if your child asks for bread, will give a stone? . . . How much more will

1. Forsyth, *The Person and Place of Jesus Christ*, 348.

2. Graham, *Where I Am*, 18, 22.

3. Placher, *Jesus the Savior*, 137.

your Father in heaven give good things to those who ask him!" (Matt 7:9, 11).

Not only does this affirm a positive and loving God, it strongly asserts the basic goodness of human fathers! Jesus appeals to fathers: don't *you* love your children? You wouldn't play a cruel trick on your child, would you? And your children trust you, don't they? In these remarks Jesus backs up the basic goodness of fathers. Elsewhere he admires mothers, children, and even Gentiles. He is affirming *people*, and also *family*, using family imagery for both God and the community of believers. Jesus tells us the truth about God, and he offers the appealing prospect of cooperating with God.

He says very positive things about people. When a scribe agrees with Jesus' articulation of the command to love God and others and then adds "this is much more important than all whole burnt-offerings and sacrifices," Jesus tells the fellow "you are not far from the kingdom of God" (Mark 12:33–34).

Some Christians are profoundly pessimistic about the human heart, but Jesus says anyone with an honest heart can receive the kingdom of God. Those who "receive the kingdom of God as a little child" will enter it (Luke 18:17). He taught that sincere faith really is possible, and is *effective*. Further, he says that people can actually *do the will* of God: "Whoever does the will of God is my brother and sister and mother" (Mark 3:35). This would make no sense if he thought that doing the will of God were impossible. He believes in the goodness of anyone who wants to do right: "the good person out of the good treasure of the heart produces good" (Luke 6:45). He tells his disciples to love, "so that you may be children of your Father in heaven ... Be perfect ... as your heavenly Father is perfect" (Matt 5:45, 48). By practicing love and mercy people are actually imitating God!

Of course, this goes against the old notion that people are evil and that God is burning with wrath against them. The gospel is meant to dispel such fearful and pessimistic views of God. "Fear not" (Luke 8:50; 12:7, 32 KJV).

5

If we follow Jesus, our entire life, our minds, and our ethics, will be forever changed.

GOD'S ATTITUDE, OUR ATTITUDE

Jesus' ethics are based on the assumption of family-relatedness between all people ("brothers") who have a common divine Parent ("Father"). His ethic was based on service rather than on patronage and self-interest. Leadership is servant-leadership, rather than the selfish exchange of favors between clients and "benefactors" (Luke 22:25). Jesus is reacting against the selfish practice of patronage in ancient society, where one only did favors in order to obligate others. People gave banquets in order to "be repaid" (Luke 14:12), but Jesus said we should hold banquets and be sure to invite "the poor . . . the lame, and the blind . . . because they cannot repay you" (14:13–14). And, really, "there is no pulling rank in this family. All allegiance is directed toward God,"[4] because "you have one teacher . . . you have one father" (Matt 23:8–9).

We are called to practice the ethics that Jesus taught. He taught that God sets out to save, to forgive, and to transform human beings. God is not being a hypocrite when God demands that *we* forgive. How unfair it would be if God demanded that we humans be more spiritual and forgiving than God is! But that is not the case. Jesus demonstrated the way of forgiveness (Luke 23:34; John 12:47).

God wants what is good for the children, as any good parent would want. Jesus shows the same attitude when he heals people and lifts them up. He healed a woman with a bent spine, saying "Ought not this woman, a daughter of Abraham whom Satan bound for eighteen long years, be set free from this bondage on the sabbath day?" (Luke 13:16). The religious people of her day were undoubtedly ashamed of this woman, and avoided her, but Jesus lifted her up, calling her a daughter of Abraham.

---

4. Thompson, *The Promise of the Father*, 108.

God cares about each person. Further, God would give spiritual blessings to us right up to the limit of our ability to receive: "God gives to all generously" (Jas 1:5). Each person will tend to develop a hunger for a *particular* quality of truth or goodness, and God wants to give us those qualities. This is the real meaning of the saying "Ask and you will receive" (John 16:24). It is not a promise of indulging every wish, but a promise that we can get some of the Godly qualities that we crave. "God . . . gives the growth" (1 Cor 3:7).

Our own giving should be modeled on God's generosity: "Freely you have received; freely give" (Matt 10:8 NIV). Ethics grows out of an understanding of God: "It is precisely the fact that the community knows and calls upon God as 'our Father in heaven' that obligates them in turn to treat each other with familial love and care."[5] To the extent that we are able, we should seek to emulate God: "Be merciful, just as your Father is merciful" (Luke 6:36). Of course, we must *believe* in the mercy and goodness of the Father if we would reflect it. What good could we reflect if we thought of God as angry and judgmental? But if we know God is forgiving, then we can be forgiving, too. In our prayer life, if we pray for our own forgiveness we should also forgive those who have sinned against us (Luke 11:4).

Forgiveness is not isolated from other life requirements. When forgiveness functions properly, it is part of what happens when people become educated and sensitive to each other, learn to develop mutual understanding, and set about to restore damaged relationships. Of course, the process doesn't work fully if all parties are not willing participants. Forgiveness works best within a religious community with a healthy level of spirituality, where people are considerate of others and are seeking to do the will of God.

As a pastor, I have observed that there is a link between what people believe about God, and how they treat each other. Problems follow when God is thought to be vindictive. That belief does damage to our ethics, stifles our spirituality, and leaves people emotionally wounded and theologically confused. Even when God is

5. Ibid., 110.

said to be a just but punishing judge, distortion occurs, since that idea generates fear. The next time someone tries to convince you of the payment-in-blood theology, take notice of how much fear and pressure that person is using to try to convince you. There is an ugly psychology that underlies atonement, and it is often communicated in a mean-spirited and bullying way.

THE NEGLECTED TEACHING

The most neglected of all of Jesus' teachings is this one: "For this I was born, and for this I came into the world, to testify to the truth. Everyone who belongs to the truth listens to my voice" (John 18:37). He came to earth to *teach truth*, to reveal God, to live out goodness, and to demonstrate spiritual beauty by implanting and nurturing love.

His revelation of truth goes beyond just his teachings. It is very much revealed in his *way of living*, since that is where he really shows the intimate trust he had in God, whom he called "Father." Whenever he says "my Father," we can sense a background of years of prayer, trusting, and communing with God. And when he speaks of "my Father and your Father" (John 20:17), he is letting us know that *we* can have that intimate experience, too. That is his greatest revelation: his life of trusting, and the faith and good will that he always practiced. By speaking of "my Father and your Father" he is showing that the Father is not out of reach. God's infinity is out of reach, God's divine power is out of reach, but a childlike relationship to our spiritual Father is *not* out of our reach.

The spiritual life that Jesus encourages will lead us to become spiritually liberated because we will actually *know truth*: "You will know the truth, and the truth will make you free . . . Everyone who commits sin is a slave to sin . . . [but] if the Son makes you free, you will be indeed" (John 8:32, 34, 36). Truth is not only spiritually liberating, but it can be mentally and socially liberating, as well. Many people have been freed from bad ideologies, oppressive groups, and false teaching when they have discovered the gospel of Jesus.

He came to live the life of truth, and then to bestow the "Spirit of Truth" after he left (John 14:17; 15:26), the Spirit that "will guide you into all the truth" (16:13). He came to bring beauty, goodness, and *living* truth to the earth. He prayed "Your kingdom come, your will be done, on *earth* as it is in *heaven*" (Matt 6:10)—to make earth less estranged from heaven!

It should be clear, then, that Jesus came to *show forth* God, not to *pay off* God. He did not come to suffer violence or to inflict it. "I do not judge anyone," he said, "for I came not to judge the world, but to save the world" (John 12:47).

Then *how* did he bring salvation? If his death is all that mattered, that would make all his teachings, his encounters, and his healings—in fact *most* of the gospel narrative—unimportant. But all these encounters and teachings *did* matter. Many people's lives were forever changed by their encounters with the *living* Jesus. We need to notice what Jesus says in these encounters. He finds saving significance in people's faith—either in God, or in him, or both. I have already mentioned the *seven times* in the Gospels where he tells people "your faith has saved you." And he never adds "dependent upon your believing in my coming death as a sacrifice." Rather, Jesus links salvation to people's spiritual choices and loyalties. He uses a woman's gratitude and love to proclaim that gratitude and love are connected with *saving faith*: "'her sins, which were many, have been forgiven; hence she has shown great love' . . . Then he said to her, 'Your sins are forgiven . . . Your faith has saved you'" (Luke 7:47–50). In this woman's encounter with Jesus, her gratitude leads to faith, and faith leads to salvation.

It is about such people as this faithful woman that he is speaking when he says "blessed are the pure in heart, for they will see God" (Matt 5:8). He affirms that the believer can "make the tree good," and that "the good person brings good things out of a good treasure" (Matt 12:33, 35).

Of course, we are not saving ourselves. It is *God* who saves. God first reached out to us, before we could ever reach out for divine truth and goodness. But we have to *respond* to this divine outreach, and Jesus, in these sayings, shows how important people's own faith experiences are. He *values* their reaching out in faith and hope.

2

WHY WAS JESUS KILLED?

Well then, one might ask: why *was* Jesus killed? I believe it was human politics, pride, and love of power that conspired to kill him. Some religious politicians felt their power was threatened by his independent teaching, and they persuaded the Roman procurator to execute him. The religious politicians happened to be Jewish, but such behavior is not a *Jewish* feature but a *human* one. Down through time, it has been common for religious leaders to take offense at independent teachers. In this case, the Sadducees, along with *most* of the Pharisees, forgot their moral principles, plotted to frame Jesus on false charges, and handed him over to the Romans to be killed. The Sadducees were the wealthy and conservative Jerusalem priests. The Pharisees were a lay religious party; they were more open-minded religiously.

Let us spell this out a little. The Sadducees did not accept anything outside the Torah (the first five books of the Bible). The Pharisees were, relatively speaking, the liberals within Judaism. They were serious laymen who followed the purity laws that applied to priests, even though they were not priests. They were more open to religious discussion and accepted the idea of an afterlife. Yet most (not all) of the Pharisees felt threatened by the influence of this independent teacher and prophet whom they had not trained. They tried to trip him up with debates, trying to get him to say something they could use against him. To be fair, some of the Pharisees rejected this plot, and a few even became disciples (Joseph of Arimathea [Luke 23:50–53] and Nicodemus [John 3:1; 7:50]). But most of the Pharisees (judging from the Gospel record) felt their prestige was at stake, and joined the conspiracy against Jesus.

Jesus dared to bypass the priestly cult system[1] (controlled by the Sadducees) when he said forgiveness of sins was freely available to all. The supposedly powerful priests were truly afraid of the power of this single man, and they stooped to the shameful act of framing him, which revealed their desperation and impotence. And by his response, that man of God revealed his spiritual power and courage.

What got Jesus killed was a cynical conspiracy between zealous conservatives and pretend liberals, along with the moral cowardice of a creepy politician (Pilate). Grimsrud says it a little differently: "Jesus died due to the combined violence of cultural exclusivism (seen in the Pharisees and focused on the issue of the law), religious institutionalism (seen in the leaders linked with the temple), and political authoritarianism (seen in the occupying Roman colonial hierarchy)."[2]

THE CONSPIRACY AND THE RESPONSE

It has to be said that the railroading and condemning of Jesus was an evil plot by people who were prisoners of their own pride and position. The irony is that Jesus came to free just such people. Jesus announced his mission as being "to proclaim freedom for the prisoners . . . to set the oppressed free" (Luke 4:18 NIV). He came *especially* to free those held captive by pride and power, and those oppressed by spiritual blindness. The *spiritual* captivity that we create for ourselves is the worst confinement. The most heartbreaking of all oppression is our own narrow-mindedness and

---

1. "Cult" refers to a repeated ritual, or a ritual system. This is the academic definition of "cult."

2. Grimsrud, *Instead of Atonement*, 21–22.

judgmentalism. The hardest prison to escape is our own mental subjugation to dogmas that we think cannot be questioned. But Jesus is the greatest jailbreaker of all time. If only the Sadducees and Pharisees had *wanted* that freedom! If only they could have seen how *bound* they were by their love of power, their pride of position, their judgmental thinking!

Jesus truly suffered. He endured the heartbreak of seeing these people harden their hearts, and he knew they were going to kill him. But he did not *have* to be murdered! That is, *God* did not intend it, and several of Jesus' parables show that. In the parable of the Tenant Farmers, we always seem to miss one key line near the beginning. The vineyard owner sends his servants to the tenants farmers, and then sends his Son in order "to collect from them his share of the produce of the vineyard" (Mark 12:2). In the NIV, this is "to collect from them some of the fruit." The vineyard owner just wants some "fruit." He is not sending his son to be killed—which would be a strange thing for a father to do! Rather, he expected the son to be respected (12:6). The owner is horrified when his son is killed. He wants only *growth* in his vineyard, not violence, and certainly not a sacrificial murder.

"Fruit" is Jesus' favorite metaphor for spiritual progress. Numerous times he uses the image of plants growing to signify spiritual growth (Matt 7:16–20; 21:43; Mark 4:20, 28; Luke 6:44). "A mustard seed . . . when it is sown it grows up" (Mark 4:31–32); "the branch cannot bear fruit by itself unless it abides in the vine" (John 15:4); "every good tree bears good fruit" (Matt 7:17). I must say it again: In the vineyard parable, Jesus says that God's Son is sent to collect some fruit, that is, to observe and encourage spiritual *growth*. Jesus did not come to earth in order to be murdered or to pay some horrible price. This parable is totally inconsistent with the idea that the Son was sent in order to be offered up as a sacrifice or a payment for human sin.

Jesus came to foster and support spiritual growth. He is all about living and bearing fruit. That is what *God* is all about, too!— *growth*, not punishment. Growth is a fundamental point throughout Jesus' teaching. It is treated as something natural and desirable:

"The earth produces of itself, first the stalk, then the head, then the full grain in the head" (Mark 4:28). We provide the conditions for spiritual growth, but God fertilizes the seed and causes the growth: "the seed would sprout and grow, [the farmer] does not know how" (Mark 4:27). This parable in Mark perfectly pictures the wonderful paradox of growth: we are like farmers who need to prepare the soil, yet the actual growth is God's doing, not our own. Spiritual growth is completely unconscious, and follows certain stages of progress that are not determined by us.

Jesus' life mission was to embody and to teach the love, goodness, and beauty of God. His purpose was not to bargain with or to persuade God in any way, but to lead us closer to a loving God. The Father already wants to give what is best for all the children. As the Epistle of James confirms: "Every good and perfect gift is from above, coming down from the Father of the heavenly lights" (Jas 1:17 NIV).

It is not God but sinful human beings who killed the Son of Man. The priests (Sadducees) desired the death of the one by whom they felt threatened, and they persuaded a cowardly Roman official to carry it out. It was not God's desire that this happen. Jesus mourns for Jerusalem, "you who kill the prophets . . . how often I have longed to gather your children together, as a hen gathers her chicks under her wings, and you were not willing" (Luke 13:34 NIV). This shows that the killing was not God's will. Jesus *would* have gathered the whole Jewish people with him in a spiritual mission, but the jealous leaders would not allow it. Instead, they killed another prophet.

Many Christians have thought of the killing of Jesus as inevitable, necessary, and even desirable (thus, "Good" Friday), but Jesus' own attitude is more sensible; he does not blame the Father for this act of violence. If Jesus thought his killing was planned by God, it would make no sense for him to *weep* over Jerusalem's unwillingness to comprehend or to recognize the time of God's visitation (Luke 19:41–44). He expresses real sorrow over the spiritual failure of Jerusalem's leaders. He feels sorrow for the people who are going to get him killed. They could have chosen to respond differently.

Once the Sadducees had put their plan into motion, Jesus recognizes that his killing is inevitable, and he warns the apostles of his coming death (Matt 16:21–26; 17:22; 20:17–19), but he says nothing about it being sacrificial or substitutionary in any way. There are nine of these passages, three in each of the Synoptic Gospels (Matthew, Mark, and Luke), and all of them are matter-of-fact warnings to his apostles about the coming tragedy. Jesus is trying to prepare the apostles for the tests they will face. He wants to forestall the grief and fear that might overwhelm them. He is *always* thinking about others, and here he is concerned about these men. In none of the nine passages does Jesus say anything about his coming death as a sacrifice. "The Son of Man must undergo great suffering, and be rejected by the elders, the chief priests, and the scribes . . . The Son of Man is to be betrayed into human hands, and they will kill him" (Mark 8:31; 9:31). These are statements about human violence, not about God's will. He anticipates his coming death, but does not speak of it as a sacrifice.

Luke the evangelist believes that the Messiah had to be put to death to fulfill what was written (Luke 22:22; 24:26–27), but the emphasis is on the predictive role of Scripture and on God's foresight, rather than on any *interpretation* of the death (as a sacrifice, a payment, etc.).

The death became *humanly* unavoidable once some powerful people conspire to kill him. One theologian asks what would happen if someone who lived wholly by love "entered hostile territory ruled by violence and domination? . . . If he kept on living by self-giving, nonviolent love, death's antithesis, that person would finally be killed."[3] So the fault is clearly that of the evildoers. Unfortunately, many people misplace the blame for the crucifixion, and then theologize upon the basis of human evildoing. Whenever people make salvation dependent on the cross, they have (probably unconsciously) made *God to blame* for the crucifixion. Let us not blame God for what *people* have done. Let us not be misled by

3. Finger, "*Christus Victor* as Nonviolent Atonement," 99.

a dreary sacrificial logic into thinking that God required sacrifice before God would forgive!

Rather, we need to recognize that good people are *often* made the target of violence, and what happened to Jesus is what has happened to many reformers, non-conformists, and prophets. "Truly I tell you, no prophet is accepted in the prophet's home town" (Luke 4:24). "Prophets are not without honor except in their own country and in their own house" (Matt 13:57). All whistleblowers are resisted by the authorities. Every courageous thinker is resented by his or her family. The creative artist is sneered at, at home. In *our* lives, this is what is meant by a prophet not being honored in the prophet's own country. It is a tragic phenomenon in human society, caused by people's hostility to reform, fear of change, and resistance to truth.

JESUS' MISSION

We must remember that Jesus came here to live a *whole* human life all the way through to its ending, *whatever* that ending might be. It turned out that his enemies decided to frame him and get him killed. A necessary part of the incarnation experience was that he *not* use miracles to escape that end, because an ordinary person could not pull off a miraculous escape. He had to experience what people experience in this often unjust and dangerous world. He drank the cup of authentic human living. As the Epistle to the Hebrews says, "Since, therefore, the children share flesh and blood, he himself likewise shared the same things . . . He had to become like his brothers and sisters in every respect" (Heb 2:14, 17).

Jesus did not escape sorrow, misunderstanding (even by his family), or severe injustice. He knows what we go through when we are despised for doing good. He knows the heartbreak of having his love rejected and his teachings misrepresented. The incarnation was indeed the divine plan, even though it meant that the Son would come like a "light shin[ing] in the darkness," a darkness that would try to overcome it (John 1:5). But it was wholly appropriate that the Creator should incarnate as a human being. "The Creator of souls came in fashion as a soul he made . . . Could the agent of creation in Godhead not appear among the persons he created?"[4]

Jesus lived a genuine human life with all the joy and sorrow it could contain, so he knows *by experience* what human life is like. He can "sympathize with our weaknesses," for he "has been tested as we are" (Heb 4:15)—actually tested much more severely than most of us will ever be. The quiet courage and determination with which he lived out his last days and accepted the fate that people had planned for him, the mercy that he showed while on the cross (Luke 23:34, 43), these are the *same* courage and mercy that he demonstrated throughout his life. His whole life, *including* the way he behaved as he was railroaded even unto death, was a revelation of God's nature.

Jesus tried to win his people, the Jewish people, over to his spiritual vision of God's will. He *would* have gathered them under his wing and have led them into a new age of spiritual truth and religious living, if they had accepted his revelation, but their leaders rejected the offer. And most people follow leaders. That is the "sheep"-like quality of people that Jesus noticed (Matt 18:12; Mark 6:34; 14:27; John 10:2). He tried to get through to these religious leaders, but, tragically, they turned against him. This was heart-breaking for him, for he knew there would eventually be dire consequences. He grieved for Jerusalem, because "you did not recognize the time of your visitation from God" (Luke 19:44). A generation after this spiritual failure, the impulses of the Jewish people led them into a nationalist rebellion, which was crushed by Rome in 70 AD.

It was sinful human action that conspired against Jesus and got him killed. Human history has been cursed with violence, scapegoating, and lust for power, even in religious institutions. This needs to be recognized and repudiated as *human* sin and not as God's fault, if we are ever to move into a time of peace, where we may be ruled by the Prince of Peace.

These facts should never be used to slander the Jewish people. When it comes to hypocrisy, murder, and treachery, so-called

4. Forsyth, *The Person and Place of Jesus Christ*, 348.

Christians have been second to none. The betrayal and killing of reformers like Jan Hus, the cruelty of both Catholics and Protestants during the Reformation, and the monstrosity of sexual molestation by clergy in our day—these show that Christians have no justification for looking down their noses at Jews. The Jewish leaders *did* let their people down by failing to recognize the time of their visitation from God. It was a failure of insight and of common decency, like many that happened before, and like many that have happened since.

The blood-atonement obsession of so many Christians is also a failure of insight. How did we have arrive at this place where so many Christians believe that God sent Jesus to be killed as a sacrifice, that his death should serve as a ransom payment to buy salvation? How did sacrificial ideas become so dominant, in the religion that grew up around the one who said "Go and learn what this means, 'I desire mercy, not sacrifice'" (Matt 9:13)? Parallel to this is the ethical question: How have we arrived at a place where Christians sometimes embody bullying and self-righteousness, in direct contradiction to everything Jesus embodied? Both of these questions involve accounting for how Christians strayed from the teaching of Jesus.

To start with the question about sacrifice, we must observe how deeply ingrained were the practice and the *concept* of sacrifice during the time when Christianity originated. And so we must examine sacrificial texts in the Old Testament. In chapters 3 and 4, I will look at the practice of sacrifice, the debate about it, and the *interpretation* of sacrifice that underlies Christian sacrificial metaphors.

3

SACRIFICIAL THINKING

Sacrifice was a widespread practice in ancient societies, often believed to be an essential part of religion. In order to understand Christian theologies of atonement, we must study the sacrificial background, primarily Jewish practices and interpretations, but also Greek and Roman traditions. It is also helpful to try to discover some of the primitive religious ideas that lie in the background of both Jewish and Gentile beliefs. The widespread ancient idea that the gods were dangerous and moody, and that sacrifice was a gift to appease the gods' anger, made sacrifice a kind of *bribe*. The Jewish priests who wrote the sacrificial texts of Exodus, Leviticus, and Numbers resisted this concept, and yet the idea of a *payment* to God was still present. Sacrifices were frequently referred to as "gifts"; they carried a certain *value*. Israelite men are told that, when they make a religious pilgrimage to Jerusalem, "they shall not appear before the LORD empty-handed" (Deut 16:16).

The burnt-offering or whole offering, which was wholly burnt on the altar, was thought of as a gift to the Lord: "an offering by fire of pleasing odor to the LORD," stated three times in Leviticus 1 (1:9, 13, 17). The offering of well-being (or peace offering) is also "an offering by fire of pleasing odor to the LORD . . . a food-offering by fire to the LORD" (3:5, 11). "All fat is the LORD's" (3:16). The ancient concept (much more ancient than Leviticus) is that God

19

is being given food, and he "eats" it by inhaling the smoke. Also present in Leviticus is a completely different purpose for sacrifice: *purification.*

ISRAELITE SACRIFICE

Israelite religion shared with its neighboring religions the idea of impurity (or "defilement," or "uncleanness"). Impurity was a kind of invisible corruption that threatened to drive away the Deity. In Babylon, Assyria, Israel, and other temple-centered cultures, rituals of purification were considered necessary to keep the deity from leaving the sanctuary or temple. Impurity and the need for purification are dominant concerns in Leviticus and Numbers, and play a major role in Exodus, as well.

The purposes of the sin offering, as found in Leviticus, were to cleanse impurity and to obtain forgiveness: "The priest shall take some of the blood of the sin-offering with his finger and put it on the horns of the altar of burnt-offering, and pour out the rest of its blood at the base of the altar of burnt-offering. All its fat he shall turn into smoke on the altar . . . Thus the priest shall make atonement on his behalf for his sin, and he shall be forgiven" (Lev 4:25–26). The blood that was daubed on the horns and at the base of the altar was considered to *purify* these installations. Forgiveness follows upon the ritual purification.

The verb that is translated "make atonement" is כִּפֶּר, *kipper.*[1] It means both "purify" and "ransom."[2] The sin-offering was understood both to *purify* and to *compensate* for wrongdoing: "You shall bring to the LORD, as your penalty for the sin that you have committed, a female from the flock, a sheep or a goat, as a sin-offering; and the priest shall make atonement on your behalf for your sin." (Lev 5:6). But a substitute—a kind of payment—could be provided: "if you cannot afford a sheep, you shall bring to the LORD, as your penalty for the sin that you have committed, two

1. Finlan, *The Background and Content of Paul's Cultic Atonement,* 36, 38–41.

2. Sklar, *Sin, Impurity, Sacrifice, Atonement,* 7, 12, 185–87.

turtle-doves or two pigeons, one for a sin-offering and the other for a burnt-offering" (5:7). The burden of sin or wrongdoing was then lifted: "Thus the priest shall make atonement on your behalf for the sin that you have committed, and you shall be forgiven" (5:10).

The primitive idea of sacrifice as a payment or compensation was still present, even when the priests tried to make it secondary. In fact, it was present in the language itself. The main Hebrew verb that is translated "to atone" is *kipper*, and it has a cognate (linked) noun *kofer*, which means a ransom or redemption payment. Thus, the concept of *payment* is linguistically built into the concept of ritual purification. In fact, sometimes the sacrifice itself is called a *kofer*, a payment. There is monetary value to a *kofer*, which occasionally can be translated as "bribe."[3]

There is also an undercurrent of violence in the *kipper/kofer*. In several stories, atonement is accomplished through killing. In Numbers, when some Israelites were taking Midianite women as partners, one priest skewered a Jewish man and a Midianite woman together (Num 25:7–8), and the Lord says that this action "turned back my wrath," and "made atonement [*kipper*] for the Israelites" (25:11, 13). In another horrific story, David has to "make expiation" (*kipper*) for Saul's killing of Gibeonites by letting the Gibeonites impale Saul's sons (2 Sam 21:3, 8–9). These stories show the culture of violence that underlies atonement. *Kipper* means purification, but it often means purification by means of payment, or even violent *payback*.

Kipper clearly means ransom or pay-off in some passages. The people offer the spoils of war to the priests in order "to make atonement" (Num 31:50). When the Lord orders a census, he tells Moses that "all of them shall give a ransom for their lives to the Lord . . . to make atonement for your lives" (Exod 30:12, 15). This is a threat of violence; it is people's *lives* that are ransomed. Even the liturgical service of the Levites has a background in killing: "I struck down all the firstborn in the land of Egypt . . . but I have

3. As in Amos 5:12; Sklar, *Sin, Impurity, Sacrifice*, 56, 58. On *kofer* in depth, see 68–75.

taken the Levites in place of all the firstborn among the Israelites ... to make atonement for the Israelites" (Num 8:17–19). The whole sacrificial system is surrounded by threats, and by a fear of what is holy.

Although the Jewish priests tried to diminish the idea of payment or persuasion in sacrifice, they did not remove it. The concept of God as violent and dangerous is a notion with great antiquity, probably in all cultures, and possibly rooted in the genuinely dangerous environment in which our ancestors grew up. The same instinctive belief underlies the thinking of many Christians. This idea has only minimal support in the New Testament, yet it "rings true" for people who *expect* God to be like an angry parent who needs to be conciliated or persuaded.

In the Torah, the Lord is pictured as very demanding: "my offering, the food for my offerings by fire, my pleasing odor, you shall take care to offer to me at its appointed time" (Num 28:2). And again: "You shall offer a burnt-offering to the LORD, a pleasing odor" (Num 29:8). That phrase, "a pleasing odor," occurs forty-two times in the Torah. The ancient idea that is showing through is that the Lord needs to be placated by being *fed* (with smoke): "They offer the LORD's offerings by fire, the food of their God" (Lev 21:6).

Even when people stopped believing that God *literally* ate the smoke, they retained the primitive idea that God was pleased with costly sacrifices. We see this in the passages where David explains to Araunah that he cannot accept his oxen for free. Rather, the sacrifice has to *cost* David something: "I will buy them from you for a price; I will not offer burnt-offerings to the LORD my God that cost me nothing" (2 Sam 24:24; see also 1 Chron 21:24).

The underlying assumption is that sacrifice is effective because it *costs* something. The idea of sacrifice as a payment or bribe persists, despite priestly efforts to emphasize purification instead. The popular attitude shows through in some of the psalms and historical narratives—the idea that costly or numerous sacrifices are impressive, and help to secure God's favor: "I will offer to you burnt-offerings of fatlings, with the smoke of the sacrifice of rams; I will make an offering of bulls and goats"; the result is: "truly God has listened" (Ps 66:15, 19). The point of "your burnt sacrifices" is that God may "grant you your heart's desire, and fulfill all your plans" (Ps 20:3–4). These psalmists seem sure that impressive acts of worship will result in divine favor: "I give you thanks, O LORD, with my whole heart; before the gods I sing your praise; I bow down towards your holy temple and give thanks to your name . . . On the day I called, you answered me" (Ps 138:1–3).

So, we see that, historically, sacrifice has undercurrents of violence, coercion, persuasion, and payback. Further, it turns out that sacrifice was a hotly debated subject. There is nothing close to a consensus about sacrifice within the pages of the Old Testament; it was not universally accepted. Let us examine this dispute within the Bible.

SACRIFICE OR MERCY?

Exodus 35 and Leviticus 1 show God instructing Moses to institute the sacrificial system. At least two of the Hebrew prophets directly challenge this story, and other prophets try to get people to relate to God without relying on sacrificial thinking. Jeremiah rejects the idea that God instituted sacrifice *at all*: "in the day that I brought your ancestors out of the land of Egypt, I did not speak to them or command them concerning burnt offerings and sacrifices. But this command I gave them, 'Obey my voice, and I will be your God, and you shall be my people'" (Jer 7:22–23). Notice how Jeremiah makes a sharp *contrast* between sacrificing and *obeying*. Many theologians try to downplay this shocking, radical position. But Jeremiah was at odds with the temple system, even mocking "these deceptive words: 'This is the temple of the LORD, the temple of the LORD, the temple of the LORD'" (Jer 7:4).

Similarly, Amos claims that there were no sacrifices in the Exodus: "Did you bring to me sacrifices and offerings the forty years in the wilderness, O house of Israel?" (5:25). The implied answer is "no," for Amos had just *contrasted* sacrifice with justice: "your burnt-offerings and grain-offerings, I will not accept them . . . But let justice roll down like waters, and righteousness like an ever-flowing stream" (5:22, 24). Sacrificing is not what God really wants. Amos and Jeremiah seem to be picking up on the view of the early prophet, Samuel: "Surely, to obey is better than sacrifice, and to heed than the fat of rams" (1 Sam 15:22). But there is a sharper edge to Jeremiah's and Amos's sayings. For them, there is not just something *better* than sacrifice, but sacrifice is not what God asked for in the first place.

And yet, the whole Torah and most of the historical books (Joshua through Esther) assume the legitimacy of the sacrificial cult. Obviously, there is a fierce debate going on, within the pages of the Old Testament, regarding sacrifice. Even among the prophets there is no unanimity, though the five greatest prophets who lived before the Babylonian exile (Amos, Hosea, First Isaiah, Micah, and Jeremiah) all have very harsh things to say about sacrificing.

Hosea's contempt is clear, when he has God saying, "I desire steadfast love and not sacrifice, the knowledge of God rather than burnt-offerings" (Hos 6:6). But he goes even further, making vicious fun of "altars for sinning" (8:11), and saying that the priests "offer choice sacrifices [but] the LORD does not accept them" (8:13; and see 9:4). He bitterly mocks the priestly privilege of eating the sacrificial meat when he says the priests "feed on the sin of my people" (4:8).

Some scholars say that the prophets were just trying to reform the sacrificial cult and raise the people's moral level, and this is certainly true of the prophets Ezekiel and Malachi, but not of the others I mentioned. Jeremiah and Hosea are not trying to *reform* sacrifice; they are attacking it. Micah is bitterly mocking the sacrificial cult when he writes: "Will the LORD be pleased with thousands of rams, with tens of thousands of rivers of oil? Shall I give my firstborn for my transgression, the fruit of my body for the sin of my soul?" (Mic 6:7). Of course not! That would be a crude attempt to buy God's favor. Each sacrificial suggestion is more bombastic than the one before. God's will stands in contrast to this whole way of thinking: "He has told you, O mortal, what is good; and what does the LORD require of you but to do justice, and to love kindness, and to walk humbly with your God?" (6:8).

Nor is the mockery confined to the prophets. One of the psalmists makes fun of sacrificial thinking, having God say: "If I were hungry, I would not tell you. . . Do I eat the flesh of bulls, or drink the blood of goats?" (Ps 50:12–13). The next psalmist affirms the point, but without mockery: "You have no delight in sacrifice" (Ps 51:16).

Notice that the prophets are not developing an alternate view of sacrifice, nor expressing an opinion on all aspects of sacrifice. They are concerned only with one problem: the popular notion of sacrifice as a way to win God's favor. It is *that* idea that our prophets and psalmists are condemning. They attack the widely held belief that expensive or massive sacrifices could persuade God to be favorable. Instead, "What to me is the multitude of your sacrifices? I have had enough of burnt-offerings of rams and the fat of fed beasts . . . bringing offerings is futile" (Isa 1:11, 13).

Given that there are whole books in the Old Testament that assume sacrifice or give instructions about the system of sacrifices, one can say that the majority position in the Old Testament is pro-sacrificial. But the moral criticism of sacrifice is a very strong and important minority position. We should not just dismiss such remarks as: "Sacrifice and offering you do not desire, but you have given me an open ear" (Ps 40:6). Listening to God is *contrasted* with sacrifice, just as in Jeremiah. A similar contrast is implied in Isaiah when his anti-sacrificial remark is followed by the advice "remove the evil of your doings from before my eyes . . . learn to do good; seek justice, rescue the oppressed" (Isa 1:11, 16–17). Instead of sacrificing, Isaiah calls for straightforward conversation with God: "Come now, let us reason together, though your sins are like scarlet, they shall be like snow" (1:17–18). Reasoning together means not only talking directly to God, but getting a response!

Although many psalmists clearly believe in sacrifice (Pss 20:3–5; 116:16–18), others critique it (Psalms 50 and 51), or say that praise is superior to sacrifice (Ps 69:30–31) or is *as good as* sacrifice ("Let my prayer be counted as incense before you, and the lifting up of my hands as an evening sacrifice," 141:2). The insistence of many prophets and psalmists that God needs honesty and mercy more than—or *instead* of—sacrifice is a very important viewpoint in the Old Testament. We could call it the prophetic viewpoint.

There was also a powerful critique of sacrifice in Greek culture. Plato attacked the assumption that the gods "are influenced by sacrifices and ... seduced by gifts ... or can be bought off."[4] Closer to Jesus' time, many "philosophers and satirists ridiculed sacrifice as an attempt to corrupt the gods."[5] Christianity grew up in a time of considerable interaction between Gentile and Jewish cultures, and these Greek views had a strong influence on early Christian debate about sacrifice.

Regarding the Bible: The reader will notice that I find serious differences in viewpoint among the biblical authors. I do not believe in a literal, word-for-word perfection of the Bible. The Bible is both a divine and a human product, but it definitely was written and shaped by fallible human beings whose own views, limitations, and cultural assumptions are present in the text. Even prophets are fallible: "the spirits of prophets are subject to the prophets" (1 Cor 14:32). We readers of the Bible are also fallible, but we *can* discern some truth, and we have an obligation to do our best. Fortunately, we have the Spirit within to help us, but that does not raise our interpretations above the level of human fallibility. We have to use our *minds* as well as our hearts to seek and to find the truth. We have to critique our interpretations and be willing to change them whenever we gain a new understanding.

It is time to see if we can discover anything about Jesus' own views on sacrifice.

JESUS' ATTITUDE

Most of the evidence shows that Jesus did not buy into the ideology and practice of sacrifice, although his view on sacrifice is not 100 percent clear. He tells one recipient of healing to go and make

4. Plato, *The Laws* 10.885C, 909B; 411, 445.
5. Young, *Use of Sacrificial Ideas*, 18.

the offering that Moses required for the healing of leprosy (Matt 8:4), although this seems to be a concession to *that* person's beliefs. Note the intimacy in the leper's approach, his kneeling, and Jesus' touching him. Jesus does not want to attack this fellow's beliefs. He was astutely attuned to people's beliefs, and he *honored* their beliefs rather than attacking them.

On another occasion, Jesus talks about leaving a gift at the altar, which probably refers to the payment that can substitute for a sacrifice. His main point, however, is not about sacrifice but about reconciliation: "when you are offering your gift at the altar, if you remember that your brother or sister has something against you, leave your gift there before the altar and go; first be reconciled to your brother or sister, and then come and offer your gift" (Matt 5:23–24). This is all about reconciliation, and only secondarily about offerings. He is saying that reconciliation is *urgent*, but ritual is not. So leave your gift, "and go; first be reconciled . . . Come to terms quickly" (5:24–25). In fact, don't even bother with the gift unless you have first fixed your relationship problem.

But these two stories *do* show that Jesus recognized the "givenness" of the system of offerings in the lives of some people. Jesus' own attitude is seen more clearly in his prophetic actions and sayings. All four Gospels show Jesus taking aggressive action in the Temple that disrupted the sale of sacrificial animals (Mark 11:15–19; Matt 21:12–17; Luke 19:45–48; John 2:13–22), and he quotes Isaiah 56:7 and Jeremiah 7:11 while doing so: "Is it not written, 'My house shall be called a house of prayer for all the nations'? But you have made it a den of robbers" (Mark 11:17).

I quote Mark not because his is the earliest Gospel, but because he probably gives the most accurate version of this event. Only Mark preserves the second part of Jesus' quote from Isaiah 56:7: "my house shall be called a house of prayer *for all peoples*" (Isa 56:7). Those italicized words are preserved in Mark, but absent from Matthew 21:13 and Luke 19:46, while John 2 does not quote Isaiah 56 at all. Mark retains the radical saying that the Gentiles should be included, and this certainly fits with Jesus' openness to the Gentiles.[6] Jesus is a prophet, and he affirms the universalizing idea of the prophet, which implies a criticism of the national exclusiveness of the priests. Further, when Jesus overturns the tables of the moneychangers and characterizes the temple as a "den of robbers" (from Jer 7:11), he is criticizing the economic burden that the sacrificial system imposes on poor people. It is hard to deny Jesus' radicalism when we look at his radical action in the temple and his quoting of two radical prophets. He does not seem to be a big fan of institutional and hierarchic religion. He quotes the prophets, and *acts* as a prophet.[7]

There is more evidence that Jesus was skeptical of the sacrificial system. The Gospels show him twice quoting Hosea's "love-not-sacrifice" passage. In Matthew 9, the Pharisees criticize him for associating with impure people (9:11). Jesus sees this purity fixation as being spiritually dishonest, and he responds by affirming *honesty*, and promoting mercy over sacrifice: "Those who are well have no need of a physician, but those who are sick. Go and learn what this means, 'I desire mercy, not sacrifice.' For I have come to call not the righteous but sinners" (9:12–13). His main point is that people must humbly recognize their spiritual *need* (that they "need a physician"). Jesus can reach you if you can admit that you are spiritually needy—that you are either "sick" or a "sinner"—depending upon how you *understand* your need. Jesus is aware that some people feel sick, and others feel sinful. In either case, you need to be honest. He can hardly help you if you consider yourself so pure that you do not need any help.

On another occasion, the Pharisees had criticized his disciples for gleaning on the Sabbath, and he scolds them for not knowing that survival needs are more important than ritual: "if you had known what this means, 'I desire mercy and not sacrifice,' you would not have condemned the guiltless" (Matt 12:7). Here, "mercy" over "sacrifice" means compassion over ritual strictness.

6. On his interacting with Gentiles and travelling to Gentile territories, see Mark 5:1; 7:24–30; Matt 8:5–13; 15:21–27; John 12:20–23.

7. A recent book emphasizes Jesus' affirmation of the prophetic value of *hesed*, or loving kindness (Drake-Brockman, *Bad Faith*).

The Pharisees' hyper-seriousness about ritual rules leads them to attack "the guiltless." Their ritualism makes them hard-hearted and merciless. When we join this passage with Matthew 9, we see Jesus affirming the legitimacy of human *need*, both material and spiritual, and rejecting religious nitpicking that is actually very unspiritual.

In another passage, there are anti-sacrificial implications in the way Jesus responds to a scribe. The scribe says "'to love [God] with all the heart, and with all the understanding, and with all the strength' and 'to love one's neighbor as oneself'—this is much more important than all whole burnt-offerings and sacrifices," and Jesus answers "You are not far from the kingdom of God" (Mark 12:33–34). Jesus is strongly affirming the scribe's allusion to a radical quote from the prophet Samuel: "Has the LORD as great delight in burnt-offerings and sacrifices, as in obedience to the voice of the LORD?" (1 Sam 15:22).

In Mark 7:10–13 Jesus opposes the Pharisaic practice of making a gift to the temple (a "qorban" or "corban"), which enabled people to withhold financial support from their aged parents, a shameful abandoning of family responsibility. The whole passage from Mark 7:1–23 is strongly critical of the ritual purity tradition, referring to it as "human precepts," "human tradition" (7:7–9), "making void the word of God through your tradition" (7:13). One could argue that this is a particular emphasis of the evangelist Mark, but one finds similar remarks in the other Gospels (Matt 15:5–9; Luke 11:39–41; John 13:10).

Jesus repeatedly identifies with the most important principles of the prophets. He restates Micah 6:8 when he advocates "justice and mercy and faith" (Matt 23:23). Here he changes Micah's "walk humbly with your God" into "faith," but that is what "faith" really means. So in Matthew and Mark, we see Jesus strongly affirming prophetic principles, but we see it also in Luke and John.

In Luke, he announces the beginning of his ministry by quoting Isaiah 61: "he has anointed me to bring good news to the poor. He has sent me to proclaim release to the captives and recovery of sight to the blind, to let the oppressed go free," and he affirms

"Today this Scripture has been fulfilled in your hearing" (Luke 4:18, 21). Throughout his ministry, he not only fulfills the promises in that passage, but affirms the prophet's hopes and values. Again he quotes Isaiah when he says the Father is drawing people to him, and "they shall all be taught by God" (John 6:45; Isa 54:13). It seems clear that Jesus sees his ministry as fulfilling many of the hopes found in Isaiah. We even find an Isaiah connection when Jesus later encounters rejection; the Fourth Evangelist sees this as fulfilling a warning from Isaiah about the hardening of hearts (John 12:38–41; Isa 53:1; 6:10).

But there is no sustained attack on sacrifice in the Jesus material comparable to Isaiah 1 or Micah 6. For the most part, Jesus simply ignores the sacrificial system and the thinking that underlies it. He offers a more direct and individual approach to God, one that is like the relationship between a child and its parent, characterized by love, learning, and growth, and not by ritual or the alleged need for purification. He seems to prefer emphasizing the positive rather than attacking the negative. The exceptions—the things he *does* attack—are hypocrisy and cruelty. These are too deadly and evil to overlook. But there does emerge from the four Gospels a consistent picture of Jesus encouraging and uplifting people, affirming the faith they already have, loving them, and teaching them about honesty and humility. He says nothing about people needing to believe in his coming death as a sacrifice.

There is a complete absence of sacrificial images in Jesus' warnings about his coming death (Mark 8:31; 9:31; 10:33; and six parallel passages). These are practical warnings designed to help the apostles cope with the traumatic effect that his death is going to have on their faith. He is worried about the apostles, so he warns them, but the warnings do not "sink in." The apostles were in denial about the danger facing Jesus and, later, they were overwhelmed with fear and despair by the arrest and crucifixion. Nor were they prepared to believe in the resurrection when the women reported their encounters with the risen Jesus.

There is a ransom saying that was attributed to Jesus, a startling and "rather isolated"[8] saying found in Mark and copied in Matthew: "to give his life a ransom for many" (Mark 10:45; Matt 20:28), but it is of doubtful authenticity. Luke 22 has the same story, the same message about unselfish service, but completely lacks the ransom saying, which is inconsistent with Jesus' teaching. The message about unselfishness ("I am among you as one who serves," Luke 22:27; "the Son of Man came not to be served but to serve," Mark 10:45; Matt 20:28), certainly fits with everything Jesus taught, but not the message about "ransom," which seems to be "coloured by the later doctrinal teaching of the Church."[9] They may have gotten the ransom idea from the Apostle Paul. The letters of Paul are fifteen and twenty-five years earlier than the writing of Mark and Matthew, respectively.

It seems that the apostles were among those "captives" of old religious thinking whom Jesus came to release: "He has sent me to proclaim release to the captives and recovery of sight to the blind, to let the oppressed go free" (Luke 4:18). The apostles were "oppressed" by their preconceptions and their biases, their tendency to retain categories of purity thinking, their resentment of Gentiles, their feelings of superiority toward women and children. Jesus was led to call them "you of little faith" (Matt 6:30; 8:26; 16:8; Luke 12:28). The way that Jesus uses this label suggests both blunt criticism and personal tenderness.

The idea of Jesus' death as a sacrifice does not originate with him but with some apostles' usage of common *cultural images* (particularly by Paul). Let us look at the development of Christian sacrificial theology.

8. Wedderburn, *The Death of Jesus*, 64; see also note 74.
9. Rashdall, *The Idea of the Atonement*, 29.

4

CHRISTIAN THEOLOGY
OF RANSOM-SACRIFICE

The first thing to notice is the absence of sacrificial ideas from the earliest apostolic teaching as reported in Acts of the Apostles (2:14–40; 3:12–26; 4:8–12). The crucifixion is mentioned many times (Acts 2:23, 36; 3:15; 4:10), but there is nothing about it being a sacrifice or a payment. The apostles emphasize the *injustice* of that killing, the *impossibility* of death having power over the Messiah (Acts 2:24, 31; 4:27), and God acting to vindicate Christ (Acts 2:32–35; 3:26; 4:10). The early focus, in their telling of the story of Jesus, was on his goodness, his teaching, his status as Messiah, the cruel injustice of his being killed, his resurrection, the coming of the Spirit, and the forgiveness of sins.

The early apostolic teaching simply did not interpret the death of Jesus sacrificially. Morality, spirituality, Christology, and the hope for the resurrection of believers were all there from the beginning, but atonement was not. Our earliest source for a Christian concept of sacrificial atonement is the Apostle Paul, who was writing in the 50s AD. In fact, there is only one verse in all of Acts that contains the atonement concept (20:28), and it is rightly attributed to Paul. Luke (the author of Acts) knew that

Paul's teaching on salvation was distinctly different from that of the other apostles (and of Jesus himself).

It is Paul who articulated the new teaching about Jesus dying as a sacrifice or a redemption payment, although he claimed to have learned these doctrines from other Christians, probably in Antioch (1 Cor 15:3).[1]

To understand the development of sacrificial theology, we have to put ourselves in the place of the apostles. The cruel railroading and killing of Jesus was a traumatizing experience for them, and it remained a "scandal" when they tried to proclaim the gospel afterwards. It is understandable that some early believers, living in a religious culture where there was powerful anxiety about sin and impurity, with a sacrificial ritual that was believed to cleanse impurity and forgive sins, would use the sacrificial metaphor to give meaning to Jesus' death. In sacrifice, there was a shedding of (animal) blood, followed by forgiveness and cleansing. This could be used as a metaphor for Jesus' death and its presumed effect. It gave meaning to an act of senseless violence.

The images that Paul used to interpret the death of Jesus as a saving event (sacrifice, redemption, and justification) were effective because they drew upon familiar parts of culture and daily life. These concepts were *already* fundamental to people's lives, not as *metaphors* (as nowadays), but as *practices*—common social institutions or transactions.

The religious practice of sacrifice was centuries old in both Jewish and Gentile cultures. It was not only a known practice, but a familiar *idea* in the lives of Jews, Greeks, and Romans. And since there was an element of blood and of purification present in ritual sacrifice, it is understandable that this familiar practice lent itself to metaphorical usage to interpret the death of Jesus.

Among other things, applying the sacrificial metaphor to the death of Jesus was a way of conferring holiness upon a thoroughly *unholy* and violent miscarriage of justice. But we no longer live

---

1. Regarding possible influences on Paul's doctrine, especially on the dying-as-a-martyr theme, see Finlan, *The Background and Content of Paul's Cultic Atonement*, 193–210.

in a culture where sacrifice is a respected ritual surrounded by an atmosphere of holiness. We no longer believe that sacrificial blood actually cleanses impurity, or that ritual sacrifice was commanded by God. We no longer get that benefit from the sacrificial metaphor. But we do need to understand how that image came to be used, and why it was so effective.

PAUL'S FOCUS

Paul understands the Messiah's death to have had a saving effect, and he uses four basic metaphors to picture it—Christ dying as a sacrifice, as a scapegoat, as a redemption payment, or as a means of justification. To some degree, each metaphor pictures *how* the death functioned, although the meanings are *suggested* rather than being *spelled out*. The sacrificial metaphor seems to make a holy event out of what was really an unholy political murder. Sacrifice implies something holy, organized, and intentional; it suggests that the will of God was functioning through it all. Scapegoat pictures sin being magically carried away from the community. Redemption speaks of rescue through a purchase of freedom. Justification implies a court proceeding with a happy outcome. Thus, all four metaphors give meaning to what was otherwise a terrible injustice and a scandal: the crucifixion. Each of these focused metaphors implies a certain logic of salvation, and sometimes people have taken this logic very literally, assuming that sin was actually carried away, or that God was somehow paid off. That is to take the implications of Paul's metaphors beyond what he intended.

Paul says "we proclaim Christ crucified . . . Our paschal lamb, Christ, has been sacrificed" (1 Cor 1:23; 5:7). This "sacrificializing" of salvation has proven to be increasingly difficult for subsequent generations. People have become anxious and confused when trying to comprehend the sacrificial logic in Paul's concept of salvation. What does it say about God? Does it mean that God was propitiated? To "propitiate" means to placate or appease, as when someone *persuades* a king to be merciful. Sometimes Paul's logic seems to suggest that God was propitiated, but in *other* places his logic works *against* that idea. In fact, both implications can occur in the same passage.

We see this in Romans 5. He says "God proves his love for us in that while we still were sinners Christ died for us" (5:8). Here, God is not at all *persuaded*. Rather, God's love and Christ's action are firmly linked, implying one motivation by both of them. Their shared purpose is to bring "grace and the free gift of righteousness" to all (5:17). And yet, Paul also says things that strongly imply propitiation. The "free gift" only happens *because* of the crucifixion: "Much more surely then, now that we have been justified by his blood, will we be saved through him from the wrath of God . . . reconciled to God through the death of his Son" (Rom 5:9–10). This seems to say that God was reconciled *only because* of "the death of his Son," that *only* by means of that death was the wrath of God averted, and that we are "justified" (pardoned) *only* "by his blood." Paul's logic turns out to be quite complicated, as he mixes the several metaphors.

It certainly seems that, if God's wrath was averted, and salvation obtained, by this violent death, then God was *appeased*, despite the non-appeasement implication of 5:8. The looming threat of wrath was a major theme in the preceding portions of the letter: "For the wrath of God is revealed from heaven against all ungodliness," and sinners "deserve to die" (Rom 1:18, 32). He warns, "you are storing up wrath for yourself on the day of wrath, when God's righteous judgment will be revealed. For he will repay according to each one's deeds" (Rom 2:5–6). Further, "There is no one who is righteous" (Rom 3:10). But then "Christ died for us," and believers are "saved through him from the wrath of God" (Rom 5:8–9). Thus, it is salvation from a *deserved* wrath.

For Paul, salvation and reconciliation are not free; they are only obtained through the Messiah's death. It is a transaction, and in First Corinthians, Paul actually calls it a *purchase*: "you were bought with a price" (1 Cor 6:20; 7:23). The word he uses for "bought" (*agorazō*) is used for purchases in the marketplace. There are other words available that mean ransoming or rescuing, but Paul chooses an unmistakably *commercial* word. However, I doubt that Paul intends this to be taken *entirely* literally, as it often is nowadays. He knows he is building metaphors, and he uses them because they are effective preaching tools. The fact that he uses *different* metaphors, each one having a different internal logic, shows that he does not intend any one of them to be taken in a materialistic and literal way.

In Romans, he chooses to use a different word for ransoming or redeeming. He says believers "are now justified by his grace as a gift, through the redemption that is in Christ Jesus" (Rom 3:24). The word for "redemption" (*apolytrōsis*) usually refers to a manumission payment (which purchases the freedom of a slave), or the ransom payment for the release of a captive.[2] Manumission and ransom payments were well-known social realities. He uses the word for such payments metaphorically, to picture what Jesus' death accomplished.

The metaphor of being "bought with a price" or "redeemed" would be powerful to people who really *were* slaves, and were hoping that someone would literally buy their freedom. "Whoever was called in the Lord as a slave is a freed person belonging to the Lord" (1 Cor 7:22). Of course, it is people's *spiritual* freedom that is meant. The idea of being bought into freedom was a vivid metaphor for that day and that audience, but for us the image of salvation being *purchased* can seem crude and morally distasteful.

The main images that Paul uses for the death of Jesus were familiar to people. Sacrifice was universally known in religious life, and redemption and justification were ideas familiar to people in their social lives. "Justification" refers to the judicial realm; it means a pardon or acquittal in court. The human soul is imagined as standing trial and being on the verge of condemnation. When Jesus obtains a pardon for the sinner, he or she is "justified by his grace" (Rom 3:24). It goes beyond mere pardon, however, all the way to reconciliation—a repair of the relationship with God: "we have been justified . . . reconciled to God . . . we have now received reconciliation" (Rom 5:9–11).

---

2. Dunn, *The Theology of Paul the Apostle*, 227.

Paul uses all these metaphors to give meaning to the death of Jesus. He is saying that Jesus died as a sacrifice (possibly bringing purification), as a redemption payment (purchasing freedom), or as justification (obtaining pardon in the heavenly court). These images "preach" well. Paul does not need to spell out all the implications. In fact, he draws back from detailed explanations, since they don't all say the same thing. When he uses the sacrifice image, it is not at all clear whether he wants the reader to imagine it as a gift/offering or as a purifying action. It *is* clear that Paul emphasizes Jesus' self-giving action and its saving effect on others, but he is not spelling out some literal *mechanics* of salvation. That is not the point. He would probably not care whether a person thinks of gift or of purification. On the one occasion where he *does* say what the "blood" accomplishes, he says it with a judicial metaphor— "we have been justified by his blood" (Rom 5:9). Paul deliberately mixes his metaphors so as to bring out the emphasis he wants. In that passage, he is stressing the unselfish giving and heroism of Jesus (the "daring to die" in 5:7), the dramatic rescue of believers ("while we were yet sinners," 5:8), and their pardon and restoration ("justified . . . reconciled," 5:9–11).

There is a strong theme of heroic martyrdom underlying all of his metaphors. Christ acts from a place of both heroism and love: "Christ died for the ungodly" (Rom 5:6). I do not call martyrdom a "metaphor" because there is no *transfer of meaning*. When we say "martyr," we always mean someone who died heroically, whereas when we say "sacrifice," we usually mean a ritually slaughtered animal. It is a transfer of meaning (a metaphor) to call the death of Jesus a "sacrifice." Martyrdom (called a "noble death") was an important theme in that age, both in Greek literature and in Jewish thought (particularly in the Maccabean literature).

Paul draws on this emotionally powerful image of noble death. But I want to emphasize that he is a persuasive preacher, not a dogmatic theologian. His emphasis is on *salvation*. He is exhorting people to believe in God's saving action through the Messiah Jesus, not constructing a rigidly logical system. When people try to force his metaphors to give a *precise* description of how salvation was obtained—a sort of *mechanics* of salvation—they mangle his thought almost beyond recognition.

The fact that Paul deliberately mixes his metaphors shows that it is the saving *result* that counts, rather than the presumed mechanics. Was Jesus' death a kind of purification ceremony? Did he die to pay a ransom price? Or did his death somehow obtain pardon for others? Well, *yes*, Paul would say. It did *something like* any one, or all three, of those. The details are not crucial. He is not building a complicated allegory of sacrifice, where every aspect of ritual sacrifice corresponds with something that happened to Jesus. He wants the reader to get the *main* point. In an important, but often mistranslated, passage, Paul blends all three of his main metaphors.

Romans 3:25

In Romans 3:24–25, Paul writes: "they are now justified by his grace as a gift, through the redemption that is in Christ Jesus, whom God put forward as a *mercy seat* by his blood, effective through faith." I will explain my correction (italicized) of the NRSV in a moment. First I want to observe that the redemption, justification, and sacrificial metaphors are all joined here. The "blood" (sacrificial) accomplishes both pardon (justification) and redemption-purchase.

Unfortunately, this passage is usually mistranslated, incorrectly calling Jesus a "sacrifice." Both NRSV and NIV mistranslate the Greek word *hilastērion* as "sacrifice of atonement," when it should be translated "mercy seat." *Hilastērion* occurs over forty times in the Greek translation of Exodus, Leviticus, and Numbers, *always* referring to the "mercy seat": the lid of the ark of the covenant. (The word in Hebrew was *kapporet*.)

The "ark of the covenant" was a box that was said to house the ten commandments (Exod 25:16, 21). The mercy seat was its lid, with two cherubim carved in gold; God was said to speak to Moses "from above the mercy seat" (Exod 25:18–22). The ark and its mercy seat were housed in the innermost room of the sanctuary, the most holy place (Exod 26:34).

In the "Israelite Sacrifice" chapter, I described the important rituals of purification, where forgiveness was treated as a consequence of purification. Now I must mention the most important of all the purification rituals. On Yom Kippur, the Day of Atonement, the high priest entered the most holy place and sprinkled the sacrificial blood on the mercy seat. Sacrificial blood, administered by the priests, was believed to have a purifying effect. This was the high point of the whole ritual purification system. In priestly belief, this purification of the mercy seat was necessary so that God would not depart from the temple.

The *hilastērion* exists within the sacrificial system, but it is a *place*, not a sacrificial *victim*. In ancient Greek literature, the word *hilastērion* is *never* used to signify a sacrificial victim, neither in "pagan" sources nor in the Greek Bible (the Septuagint). This is one of the things proven by Daniel Bailey, who has done the most detailed study of the term *hilastērion*.[3]

A related word, *hilasmos*, can indicate a sacrificial victim, and that word is used in 1 John 2:2 and 4:10, correctly translated as "sacrifice."[4] But in Rom 3:25, Paul uses the word that signifies the *place* of atonement, not the sacrificial *victim*, so "sacrifice of atonement" is a mistranslation.[5]

Christians, even scholars, sometimes see what they *expect* to see. They import ideas that they have found in *other* passages, and scholarly interpretations of Paul's theology with which they are familiar. But Paul here is saying something unique. He is saying that God put forward Jesus as a (new) mercy seat of faith through the sprinkling of his blood. The early English Reformer, William Tyndale, got it right when he translated it "a seat of mercy."[6]

---

3. Bailey, "Biblical and Greco-Roman Uses of *Hilastērion*." I rely on Bailey's dissertation in my discussion in Finlan, *Problems with Atonement*, 37–41.

4. *Hilasmos* is acceptably translated as "sin-offering" in the Greek translation of Ezekiel 44:27.

5. Hultgren also supports the translation of *hilastērion* as "mercy seat" (*Paul's Gospel and Mission*, 59–61).

6. Text taken from http://www.biblestudytools.com/tyn/romans/3.html.

Paul's metaphor refers to the most important ritual action at the holiest ritual location on the holiest of holy days, the Day of Atonement. Since it is a place where sacrificial blood is sprinkled, Paul's metaphor fits within the sacrificial *realm*. By no means am I denying that the *hilastērion* is part of the geography of sacrifice. I am only pointing out that it is a *place*, not a ritual victim. The reader may think I am being picky, but this is an important distinction. Translation needs to be *accurate*. Inaccurate translation contributes to misunderstanding.

Paul is more sophisticated and wide ranging in his use of metaphors than some scholars allow. Here he makes Christ the mercy seat, where ritual atonement was accomplished. Elsewhere he makes him the sin offering (Rom 8:3) or the scapegoat (2 Cor 5:21). Translators who insist on "sacrifice" in Rom 3:25 are narrowing down Paul's metaphorical range, forcing Jesus to be a sacrificial victim, and that *alone*. Let Paul be Paul!—by which I mean, let him use the various *different* metaphors that he *does* use.

Paul's main point is to show that God, Jesus, and the Spirit all work together to *save* people and give them new life, and that the death and resurrection of the Messiah are the key moments in that salvation process. Paul does, however, make everything hinge on the crucifixion (in some passages) or on the crucifixion *and* the resurrection (in other passages). Some of his metaphors cannot help but imply a purchase: "you were bought with a price" (1 Cor 6:20), the price being Jesus' death: "obtaining salvation through our Lord Jesus Christ, who died for us" (1 Thess 5:9–10). The believer, then, has to feel deeply indebted. If he "was handed over to death for our trespasses" (Rom 4:25), then we are to blame. If "Christ died for our sins" (1 Cor 15:3), then we are guilty.

Transformation

It is time that we accept that Paul was not perfect, and not all his metaphors are helpful to our spiritual lives now. Our concept of God the Father would be improved if we could distance ourselves from the sacrifice, purchase, and scapegoat metaphors, while retaining Paul's teachings about the *new life* that God gives: "we too might walk in newness of life" (Rom 6:4); "he who raised Christ from the dead will give life to your mortal bodies" (Rom 8:11). There is no other author who gives such a vivid description of the new identity gained by believers: "in Christ Jesus you are all children of God through faith" (Gal 3:26); "it is that very Spirit bearing witness with our spirit that we are children of God" (Rom 8:16). This is the good news: that Jesus and the Spirit tell us that we are the children of God!

These teachings are fully consistent with Jesus' own teaching. The problem is not with Paul's teaching on love, loyalty, or Spirit, but with his hyper-dramatic investment of meaning in the death of Jesus, much of which was communicated through metaphors. But it is wrong to take Paul's metaphors entirely literally. We should see them as teaching tools meant to illustrate that Jesus brought forgiveness and showed the new way of living by faith. Paul is the original New Age teacher!—the new age in Jesus. There is a new way to live "now that faith has come" (Gal 3:25); "you are not under law but under grace" (Rom 6:14). Religious living has a new emphasis: "For freedom Christ has set us free" (Gal 5:1). Freedom is not a strong value in most of the Old Testament, but now it has become a *premier* value because Jesus has set us free from fear. This changes the way we think and live: we are to be motivated by a *renewed heart* rather than by fear of God. It is not just loyalty to a law, but receptivity to the Spirit. With the freedom of the renewed heart comes increased personal responsibility. More freedom, more responsibility. Freedom and maturity, in Paul's teaching, are inseparable.

If we look at Paul in this way, if we notice his own emphasis on the Spirit and spiritual *living*, if we hear what he says on freedom, renewal, and ethical consideration for others, then we will appreciate him, and will cease to take his metaphors so rigidly, so literally.

Paul's call for ethical sensitivity in the church is unmatched: "through love become slaves to one another" (Gal 5:13); "Let love be genuine; hate what is evil, hold fast to what is good; love

one another with mutual affection; outdo one another in showing honor" (Rom 12:9–10). We could put "respect" where he has
"honor." What if respect and affection were the main attitudes that
you encountered when you went to church?

Paul envisions (for he has *experienced*) the believer having a moral and motivational *change*. The believer must be freed
not only from sin, but from the *desire* to sin, from the *appeal* of
sin (Rom 6:22; 8:10, 14). That is *real* freedom; that is an actual
repair of the human being, not just an escape from punishment.
Evangelicals sometimes think of salvation as escape rather than
as transformation. A great theologian more than a hundred years
wrote: "it is God's aim . . . to save men from sin, not from penalty."[7]

This is a real-life transformation. Paul speaks from profound
experience when he writes "where the Spirit of the Lord is, there
is freedom" (2 Cor 3:17). We need to learn about *that* from him.
No one describes spiritual metamorphosis as profoundly as Paul
does: "be transformed by the renewing of your minds, so that you
may discern what is the will of God—what is good and acceptable
and perfect" (Rom 12:2). This fits with what Jesus taught about our
ability to do the will of God (Mark 3:35; John 7:17). But Paul goes
into more detail about the gradual, step-by-step transformation
into a likeness to Christ: "all of us . . . are being transformed into
the same image from one degree of glory to another; for this comes
from the Lord, the Spirit" (2 Cor 3:18). This means believers are
being transformed into the image of the "Lord," which, for Paul,
means Christ. This is astonishing! Believers are being transformed
to resemble Jesus! It tells us that we will be passing through *stages*
in our spiritual development, unification, and learning, so that we
may become more Christlike, more self-giving, and of service to
all our fellows, both here and hereafter.

There will be a real moral change. The believer can say that he
has "a righteousness" that is not "my own . . . but one that comes
through faith in Christ, the righteousness from God based on
faith" (Phil 3:9). We will be ready for Judgment Day: "so that on
the day of Christ you may be pure and blameless, having produced

7. Bowne, *Studies in Christianity*, 193.

the harvest of righteousness that comes through Jesus Christ" (Phil 1:10–11).

God's life giving extends all the way to what can be called the divinization or deification of the believer—the taking on of holy, spiritual, and incorruptible qualities. Most of this process will take place in the afterlife, after we have received a "spiritual body" (1 Cor 15:44). Paul insists that there are different kinds of bodies. "Not all flesh is alike," he says, "there are heavenly bodies and earthly bodies" (1 Cor 15:39–40), and they are *not* the same. They differ in their degree of glory: "the glory of the heavenly is one thing, and that of the earthly is another" (1 Cor 15:40). The physical body is like a seed that is sown in the ground; the spiritual is like a plant that miraculously sprouts forth to new life. "It is sown in weakness, it is raised in power. It is sown a physical body, it is raised a spiritual body" (15:43–44). In case you didn't get his point, he repeats it: "If there is a physical body, there is also a spiritual body" (15:44b). First comes the physical, then the spiritual (15:46). Only the spiritual body can live in the next life; "flesh and blood cannot inherit the kingdom of God" (15:50).

Even though Paul goes on insistently and at some length about this, many Christians have been unable to accept the idea of a new body, a spiritual body. It is hard for people to accept something they cannot see. People tend to identify with *this* body. And so, most Christians insisted on believing in the resurrection of the *material* body, and Paul's view (unfortunately) became the minority opinion within Christianity. Even Luke and John miss the point, insisting that Jesus' resurrected body was physical (Luke 24:40–43; John 20:27). Luke and John are writing thirty-five and forty-five years after Paul, respectively. In the period after the writing of Matthew (around 80 AD) but before the writing of Luke and John, there had arisen an accusation that Christians were seeing ghosts, and Luke and John are concerned to counter this accusation.

Once again, I think we have to accept that the Bible represents the viewpoints of many different *human* authors. "The spirits of prophets are subject to the prophets" (1 Cor 14:32). The writings are God-inspired, but in every case the inspiration passes through a human mind, encountering all the biases, worries, values, and assumptions that exist in that person's mind. And so, we readers have to use our discernment. We have to do our best to discover the truth through the use of our spiritual intuition, reason, personal experience, and historical knowledge. Our feeling for, and knowledge of, Jesus should be our primary interpretive guide. I agree with Sharon Baker's principle for reading the Bible: "We need to make his life and teachings the lens through which we interpret the Bible."[8] And from another theologian: "The love commandments of Jesus take priority over . . . all other ethical injunctions that are not derived from them."[9] The spirituality, the values, and the actions of Jesus are our best guide. Through him, "the veil is removed" (2 Cor 3:16). But this is not a magic formula; we still need to use our critical faculties, along with our spiritual insight.

I find Paul's teachings on life after death to be more coherent and informative than any other author's. Our *personalities* will survive beyond the death of these material bodies, but we will need different life vehicles, ones that are appropriate to the sphere in which we are going to live. Heaven is not a place of idleness, but a place of constant *growth*, and we will need bodies that can function in a spiritual environment. In fact, spiritual growth is the principle that unites *this* life with the afterlife. Growth is the law of life. God wants to see us grow, as *any* good parent would.

Paul's teachings are an important channel for the teachings of Jesus, especially on this subject of believer transformation and the afterlife. The main problem is Paul's peculiar idea of a transaction taking place at Christ's death. He used metaphors that were effective for preaching, but the problem is that metaphors have their own afterlife, especially for the multitudes of believers who take the metaphors too literally, who think that salvation was obtained through an actual payment, even through the purchasing power of *suffering*. Bowne hit the nail on the head, regarding Paul's metaphors: "The theorists were bent on saving the language, and failed

8. Baker, *Executing God*, 87.

9. Thatcher, *Theology and Families*, 45.

to note its figurative and non-absolute character."[10] The metaphor is not the message, but the *carrier* of a message. God's open invitation, God's desire to save, and Jesus' revelation of the character of God—*these* are the message.

The Absence of Atonement in Luke and James

The earliest books of the New Testament are the letters of Paul. His ideas influenced a number of other New Testament authors, but the atonement idea never won over Luke or James. Luke wrote Acts as well as the Gospel, so there are three important New Testament books that do not conform to Paul's centering of salvation in the cross. Luke, Acts, and James do not place the moment of salvation at the crucifixion.

I agree with those who say that Luke's gospel originally contained no hint of atonement, even in the eucharistic text, which originally had no reference to blood. In Luke 22:17–18, Jesus raises the cup and says he will not drink it again until the kingdom of God comes. Then he speaks over the bread, and finally he says that the hand of the betrayer is on the table with him (22:19a, 21). That is what Luke wrote. Many scholars (and I) believe that someone inserted a verse and a half, which reads: "'which is given for you. Do this in remembrance of me.' And he did the same with the cup after supper, saying, 'This cup that is poured out for you is the new covenant in my blood'" (Luke 22:19b–20). This seems to be based on the wording in First Corinthians (1 Cor 11:24–25). The question is whether these words were present in Luke, and were then removed by a copyist (unlikely), or were added to the manuscript by a copyist (more likely, I will argue).

The apparent addition creates a clumsy movement from cup to bread and back to cup again. It is absent altogether from the oldest translations of Luke (in Latin, Syriac, and Boharic), from the earliest church lectionaries (scheduled readings for church services), and from the oldest Western Greek manuscript (known

10. Bowne, *Studies in Christianity*, 130.

as "D").[11] For these and other reasons, the great nineteenth century scholars Westcott and Hort argued that this verse and a half
were inserted, and that manuscript D (from which they are absent)
should be trusted.[12] Many scholars still support their view, although
just as many oppose it, often giving very weak arguments, such as
that the "blood" wording was omitted by accident, or from a desire
to hide the eucharistic wording from unbelievers.[13] Westcott and
Hort note "the extreme improbability that the most familiar form
of the Words of Institution, agreeing with St. Paul's record, should
be selected for omission."[14]

Certainly the manuscript copyists, even those who had this
passage available, did not know what to do with it. The manuscript
history shows extraordinary uncertainty about where this passage—or *part* of this passage—should go. It occurs in several longer or shorter forms and in various different locations in ancient
Greek manuscripts. It eventually became settled and standardized
at 22:19b–20. The insertion was probably to make Luke conform
to the wording that was becoming common in church liturgies.
But communing in the blood is completely alien to Luke's thinking. He nowhere speaks of any notion of a covenant in blood or a
ritual remembering of Jesus' blood. He does make reference to the
Eucharist, but it is "the breaking of bread" (Acts 2:42, 46; similarly,
Luke 24:30). He says "we met to break bread" (Acts 20:7).

Luke does not rely on Paul's cross-based soteriology (teaching on salvation), but places salvation in the life-giving power of
Jesus himself, in his *whole* life, his resurrection, and the Spirit that
he sent. Luke does know Paul, and knows about his atonement
teaching. In Acts 20:28, Luke shows Paul making an atonement
statement ("the church of God that he obtained with the blood of
his own Son"), but he does not make Paul's atonement concepts
the basis of his *own* understanding. He allows *Paul* to say it. Luke

11. Ehrman, *The Orthodox Corruption of Scripture*, 197–99, 204–8.

12. Westcott and Hort, *Introduction to the New Testament*, Appendix,
63–64.

13. Rightly rejected by Ehrman, *The Orthodox Corruption of Scripture*, 208.

14. Westcott and Hort, *Introduction to the New Testament*, Appendix, 63.

emphasizes Jesus' innocence. "The death of Jesus in Luke-Acts is not a death that effects an atoning sacrifice. It is the death of a righteous martyr who has suffered from miscarried justice."[15] Luke simply does not see the death of Jesus as the event that made forgiveness possible. People receive forgiveness through the *person* of Jesus (Acts 5:31; 13:38–39) or through *faith* in him (Acts 10:43; 13:39; 26:18), but not because of the crucifixion.

For Luke, salvation comes from God's saving intention, Jesus' creative and healing power, the bestowal of the Spirit, and the human desire to cooperate with God, manifested as repentance and believing in Jesus. Luke's is the longest Gospel and the only one that mentions the author's efforts to gather information by consulting eyewitnesses and earlier written accounts (1:1–4). It seems that Luke has understood the historical Jesus more clearly than the other evangelists, at least on this point.

The Epistle of James (traditionally understood to be written by James, the Lord's brother) also does not connect salvation to the death of Jesus. In fact, the death of Jesus is not mentioned at all, and it does not *need* to be mentioned. Rather, salvation is linked to getting rid of "sordid" motives and deceitful hearts (James 1:21, 26), joining faith to good deeds, receiving wisdom (2:14–17; 3:13), making peace, trusting in God (3:17–18; 4:7), and practicing prayer and confession (5:15–16). Salvation, for James, is based on God's love and the human being's spiritual loyalty and wisdom. "If any of you is lacking in wisdom, ask God, who gives to all generously and ungrudgingly" (Jas 1:5). One can almost hear the echo of Jesus' voice in what James writes: "Humble yourselves before the Lord, and he will exalt you" (4:10; see Luke 14:11; 18:14). "Do not speak evil against one another . . . pray for one another" (4:11; 5:16; see Matt 5:22, 44). James puts the emphasis on his brother's moral and spiritual teachings—on truth and righteousness, and especially on *living* the truthful and righteous life: "Just as the body without the spirit is dead, so faith without works is also dead" (James 2:26).

---

15. Ehrman, *The Orthodox Corruption of Scripture*, 201.

PAUL'S SUCCESSORS

As we saw, Paul also transmits much of the teaching of Jesus, and touches on a wide range of spiritual subjects. But his atonement teaching was a major part of what he handed on. We need to look at the legacy of Paul, first on the theme of atonement, then on other themes.

The process that Paul set in motion—the blending of sacrificial, redemption, and justification metaphors for Jesus' death—is taken even further in the next set of writings, the "Deutero-Pauline" epistles, that is, those written by successors of Paul (and sometimes attributed to Paul). In those letters, the images are simplified into the atonement-purchase concept: "In him we have redemption through his blood" (Eph 1:7). "He . . . gave himself for us that he might redeem us from all iniquity" (Titus 2:14). The idea is that Christ is the mediator or negotiator between humanity and God: "there is also one mediator between God and humankind, Christ Jesus, himself human, who gave himself a ransom for all" (1 Tim 2:5–6).

Paul's influence even entered the stream of writings associated with the name of Peter: "You were ransomed from the futile ways . . . with the precious blood of Christ, like that of a lamb without defect or blemish" (1 Pet 1:18–19). Again, what is the sacrificial death said to accomplish? The death is said to *ransom*.

With the successors of Paul, sacrifice is not only blended with ransom-redemption, it is *subordinated* to it. Paul's diversity of metaphors gets simplified into a ransom payment. Today, when Christians hear the word *sacrifice*, they think of the logic of payment or ransom. And suffering is part of what makes the ransom payment valuable, at least for the author of the Epistle to the Hebrews. "It was fitting that God . . . should make the pioneer of their salvation perfect through sufferings" (Heb 2:10). "Jesus also suffered outside the city gate in order to sanctify the people by his own blood. Let us then go to him outside the camp and bear the abuse he endured" (Heb 13:12–13). This plays into the hands of an unhealthy belief in the necessity of suffering.

The richness of theological thought that is found in Paul is narrowed down when the redemption/purchase idea becomes dominant, among his successors. Many ideas that are prominent in Paul, such as believer transformation by the Spirit, and freedom joined with obedience, become secondary. Some ideas, such as Christian prophecy (1 Cor 13:9; 14:1–5), or sharing in the sufferings of Christ (Rom 8:17; Phil 3:10), are dropped altogether. Obedience and conformity take the place of creative and transformative freedom. And simple atonement slogans take the place of the complex and multi-layered images of Paul.

But ransom and atonement were only a part of the Christian discussion. This book has a focus on atonement, so I have followed that thread, but in fact, many Christian writings in the early centuries did not at all make atonement the centermost teaching. As Christianity expanded throughout the Mediterranean world, what received primary attention from most of the leading thinkers was the message of spiritual transformation.

The Greek Patristic Period

It may be hard for a twenty-first century Christian to imagine a period of Christian history where the central focus was *not* a message about Jesus dying as a substitute for others, but that is the case during the Greek Patristic period, the time of the Greek Fathers, from about 150 to 450 AD. Throughout the Greek Patristic period the main concerns were Christology (who Jesus was and is), ethics (how Christians should live), and spirituality (prayer and spiritual experience). There is almost a complete "absence of the cross in early Christian art"; the main symbols used were the palm branch, the Good Shepherd, Jonah in the fish, boat, lamb, anchor, fish, vine and grapes, although one or two of these could be "a cryptic sign of the cross."[16]

---

16. Young, *Construing the Cross*, 75–77. The oldest inscriptions of the cross are from "the early 3rd century AD" and from "the second half of the third century" (Longenecker, *The Cross before Constantine*, 75, 81).

Two of the greatest theologians of this period, Origen and Athanasius, focused on the person and divinity of Christ, and the promise of divinization: the spiritual transformation of believers into the likeness of Christ. They sought to develop what they find in the New Testament, such as the teaching that "you may ... become partakers of the divine nature" (2 Pet 1:4 RSV).

Origen of Alexandria (mid-third century) put the emphasis on Christ's *whole life*, and especially the resurrection, the moment when death was defeated. Christ won a cosmic war against the devil; he went down into the devil's realm, preached to the spirits in prison, and freed them (1 Pet 3:19).[17] The incarnation of the Word had a transformative effect upon all believers. "Justification" really meant being morally transformed: "being made actually righteous."[18] That, too, was due to Christ's influence. Christ "is 'the pattern of the perfect life,' the exemplar of true virtue into Whose likeness Christians are to be transformed,"[19] inspiring and teaching believers to practice forgiveness and penitence.[20] Jesus had a *transformative* effect upon human nature itself: "With Jesus human and divine nature began to be woven together, so that by fellowship with divinity human nature might become divine."[21]

A century later, Athanasius took up these same ideas. "He became man that we might be made God."[22] Athanasius would use some traditional atonement language, and then turn toward the divinization idea: "When he offered His own temple and bodily instrument as a substitute for the life of all ... through this union of the immortal Son of God with our human nature, all men were clothed with incorruption."[23] Origen and Athanasius can

17. Rashdall, *The Idea of the Atonement*, 261.

18. Ibid., 273.

19. Origen, *Contra Celsum* 8.17; quoted by Kelly, *Early Christian Doctrines*, 184.

20. Rashdall, *The Idea of the Atonement*, 275.

21. Origen, *Contra Celsum* 3.28; in Kelly, *Early Christian Doctrines*, 185.

22. Athanasius, *On the Incarnation of the Word* 54; Grensted, *A Short History of the Doctrine*, 81.

23. Athanasius, *On the Incarnation of the Word* 9; p. 35.

be credited with realizing the revolutionary implications of the incarnation—the idea that the Divine lived a life among us, giving us new potentials for transformed living.

Jesus fashioned the parable of a woman leavening a whole lump of dough with a few sprinkles of leaven (Matt 18:33), to help us imagine that the mass of humanity, permeated by a few good sprinkles, will *rise*, as leavened bread rises. Jesus is saying that a few spiritually reborn people can have an uplifting effect on the whole population. The church father Gregory of Nazianzus finds new meaning in this parable when he says that the incarnation leavened the whole human race.[24] The divine Son came into humanity, and humanity is forever changed.

This Gregory is also the one who coined the word *theōsis*,[25] which eventually became the standard term for this process of the divinization of believers. Atonement concepts were still part of the conversation, but they were not the *controlling* ideas among the Greek fathers. *Theōsis* has remained a central theme in the Orthodox Churches to the present day. It was largely suppressed in the Western churches, which chose to focus instead on sin, punishment, and atonement, but *theōsis* is being rediscovered now by Catholics and Protestants.

Augustine

Possibly because of legalistic Roman thinking, the Latin church fathers have a very strong emphasis upon law, sin, penalty, punishment, and atonement. Augustine, the most influential of these theologians, even used Roman legal terminology: language of penalty, substitution, satisfaction, expiation. "He took the penalty owing to our sin upon himself."[26] "God has received satisfaction

---

24. Gregory of Nazianzen, "Epistle 101," in NPNF 2:7:441.

25. Oration 4.71; see Russell, *Doctrine of Deification in the Greek*, 214.

26. Augustine, *Contra Faustum Manichaeum* 14.7; from Kelly, *Early Christian Doctrines*, 393.

and has bestowed pardon . . . [T]he essence of the redemption lies in the expiatory sacrifice offered for us by Christ."[27]

It is Augustine who gives us "original sin," taking it so literally that he taught "that an infant was tainted in the moment of conception itself, contaminated by Adam's sin."[28] Babies are sinful and must be assumed to be damned.[29] Some claim that Augustine's main reason was to insist that infant baptism was necessary,[30] but this hardly mitigates the harsh judgmentalism of the God that he imagines.

Much of Augustine's theology seems to have a psychological and experiential basis. As a boy, he was severely beaten by his teachers. In fact, "he was unable to cry out during the beatings for fear that he would be beaten even more severely."[31] The punishment was so cruel that Augustine later compared it to torture, and yet "his parents mocked him when he showed them the stripes on his back and sought their sympathy"; he was "laughed at"![32] I think that heartless response was at least as abusive as the beatings themselves.

However, as abuse victims often do, he later justified this cruel treatment, confusing it with love, and blaming himself for not studying hard enough and for rebelling against his teachers.[33] This cruelty seriously damaged Augustine, wounding him psychologically, and warping his thinking. He developed a "tendency toward excessive self-reproach," sorrow, and shame.[34] One heart-breaking by-product of the mistreatment of children is that "we have turned to religion to find therein the legitimations for adults' assault

27. Kelly's summary of *The City of God* 10.22 and other passages (*Early Christian Doctrines*, 392).

28. Miller-McLemore, *Let the Children Come*, 69–70.

29. Bartlett, *Cross Purposes*, 59–60; Kelly, *Early Christian Doctrines*, 363, 366.

30. Miller-McLemore, *Let the Children Come*, 70.

31. Capps, *The Child's Song*, 27.

32. Ibid., 29, 22.

33. Ibid., 19, 23.

34. Ibid., 26.

against the spirit of the child"; Augustine was one whose "heart [was] crushed and broken."[35] Actually, God can do great work with a broken heart. I think it's fair to say that God did great work with Augustine, despite the negative effect of some of the latter's teaching. Sadly, Augustine was never able to recognize how his own thinking was damaged by the psychological abuse he suffered. His woundedness imprinted itself on the doctrine that he handed on.

The Blood Libel

When the concept of a violent God has been accepted within a culture for a long period of time, it can produce some very unhealthy results. I am going to look now at a subject that most writers on atonement overlook: the strange explosion of anti-Semitism and paranoia that erupted from the eleventh to fifteenth centuries in Europe, which shows a strong undercurrent of anxiety about the atonement teachings of the church.

For a long time, European Christians had blamed the Jews for the killing of Christ, and this resentment and other religious-political grudges were growing in the late eleventh century. This is when the First Crusade was organized. Anthony Bartlett points out that the Crusade provided an opportunity for revenge, because religious feelings were joined with a "warrior ethos," leading to a wave of "meritorious violence."[36] The very first military actions of the Crusade were attacks on Jewish communities in France and Germany, which killed more than a quarter of the Jewish population there[37] before any action was taken against the *stated* enemy, the Turks.

Backed up by an atmosphere of militarism and a perception of Christian culture being under threat, Christians acted out their "vendetta" against the Jews.[38] We see the psychological motiva-

35. Ibid., 36.
36. Bartlett, *Cross Purposes*, 103.
37. Ibid., 106.
38. Ibid., 108–9.

tions becoming more obvious in events of fifty years later. That is when a conspiracy theory emerged that accused Jewish communities of kidnapping and killing Christian children. The theory seems to have originated in England, with the death of William of Norwich in 1144. William was a Christian boy, whose body was found in the woods, bearing stab wounds. Some of William's relatives claimed that Jews had kidnapped and killed him, but most of the townsfolk put no stock in these allegations. Five years later, a monk named Thomas of Monmouth moved to the area, and he became obsessed with the case. He wrote a book alleging that there was an international Jewish cabal that met before Passover each year to decide where to abduct a Christian child, that England was chosen that year,[39] and that William was crucified with "many and great tortures," dying with "streams of blood" running down his body.[40] In this alleged crucifixion and ritual blood-usage, there is a grotesque echo of the atonement idea. A minor cult grew up that revered William as a saint. In the following decades, there were ritual murder accusations at several locations in England, in France, and Germany, and a number of Jews were accused, tortured, and killed.[41]

There was a significant heightening of distress among Christians after 1215, when the Catholic Church promoted the doctrine of transubstantiation, teaching that the eucharistic bread and wine became the actual body and blood of Christ. Thus, Christians were literally eating Christ's flesh. Guilt and confusion about this doctrine is reflected in the rise of accusations against Jews making evil religious use of blood. In 1235, in the German town of Fulda, Jews were accused of murdering five children and draining their blood for ritual usage. Fortunately, the emperor Frederick II absolved the Jews of the accusation, pointing out that Jewish law prohibited even the use of animal blood, and that there was no reason for them to take such a risk.[42] Unfortunately, this did nothing to stop

39. Goldstein, *A Convenient Hatred*, 75–77.
40. Ibid., 78; Rappaport, "The Ritual Murder Accusation," 306.
41. Holmes, "The Ritual Murder Accusation in Britain," 102.
42. Goldstein, *A Convenient Hatred*, 84–85.

the rapid spread of such rumors throughout France and Germany. Oftentimes, lies and rumors travel faster than the plain facts.

Before long there was a widespread myth about Jews stealing eucharistic hosts, torturing the hosts with knives until blood flowed from the hosts, and putting the blood to nefarious use. Sometimes an apparition of Christ would appear in the wafer.[43] Such accusations led to riots and to the killing of many Jews in Germany.[44]

Why such an extreme reaction, and why those particular details? They reveal Christian horror about the notion of consuming Christ's body. The experience evoked disgust since it meant Christians were committing a kind of "symbolic cannibalism."[45] But Christians could not speak this aloud, so they projected their anxiety outward onto a scapegoat community. The level of panic and rage shows that this problem had deep psychological roots. The theory that it was simply an envy of Jewish wealth is quite superficial. Monetary envy is far less explosive psychologically than are deep religious guilt and fear.

The doctrine of the Eucharist as ritual flesh-eating and blood-drinking created enormous distress and suppressed rage in Christians, which could not be brought to conscious awareness. But rage could safely be projected outward onto the alleged "Christ-killers," and this led to a wave of violence throughout Europe, from Spain to Russia. In towns and cities where these accusations occurred, local Jews were arrested, tortured, and forced to confess exactly what they were *expected* to confess: either the kidnapping of Christian children to drain their blood, or the stealing of hosts to desecrate them. Often there was a monk or cleric who "whips up the mob's frenzy"; after revenge is taken on the local Jews, the dead Christian child becomes a martyr in the popular mind.[46] The accusations

---

43. Hsia, *The Myth of Ritual Murder*, 50–56.

44. Goldstein, *A Convenient Hatred*, 86–87.

45. Dundes, "The Ritual Murder or Blood Libel," 354.

46. Schultz, "The Blood Libel," 290.

often arose in Easter season, "a period of maximum or intensified guilt feelings on the part of Christians."[47]

But the ritual that *actually* lay in the background was the Christian one, involving blood-symbolism and the interpretation of the death of Christ as a ritual murder. The truly horrible doctrine was that an angry, sacrifice-demanding God had caused the crucifixion of his innocent Son, and then required believers to eat his flesh and drink his blood. Actually what they drank in were guilt and self-loathing. Self-hatred and God-hatred are too dangerous to utter, so the psychological remedy of blaming a scapegoat is chosen. That the anxiety was centered on the Eucharist is shown by the breathlessly told stories of the kidnapping and torturing of eucharistic hosts, and occasionally of a miraculous revenge taken by the eucharistic host.

The psychological term for this kind of projection is "projective inversion," used by Alan Dundes in his masterly study.[48] One's unadmitted revulsion and painful guilt are banished by being projected onto others. What underlies the projection is the shame that Christians feel about their own blood ritual.

Educated people often resisted the blood libel, including a number of popes (Innocent IV, Gregory X, Paul III) and some reformers (the Dutchman Hugo Grotius and the German Andreas Osiander).[49] We, too, need to be educated, and to reject vendetta, superstition, and hateful rumors. The blood libel still persists in Russia and other communities.[50] It is time that we recognize the role that unhealthy atonement teaching plays in the psychopathology of anti-Semitism. Christian shame and fear help to drive anti-Semitism.

47. Dundes, "The Ritual Murder or Blood Libel," 356.

48. Ibid., 352–54. Schultz, in the same collection, affirms "the projective nature of this accusation" ("The Blood Libel," 289–90).

49. Dundes, "The Ritual Murder or Blood Libel," 359; Hsia, *The Myth of Ritual Murder*, 131, 135–43.

50. Wikipedia, "Blood Libel," in the section "20th Century and Beyond."

Luther

Martin Luther in the sixteenth century attacked the Roman church for its oppressiveness and its non-biblical teaching, and he became the fountainhead of the Reformation. This move was necessary for the sake of spiritual freedom, but Luther's theology had some serious problems. Many people in those days believed in a severe and punishing God, but Luther intensified those beliefs beyond anyone else.

The cruelty I noted in Augustine's theology is heightened by Luther. He dismisses the possibility of free will: "We do everything of necessity, and nothing by 'free-will'"; he felt everyone "has no 'free-will', but is a captive, prisoner and bondslave, either to the will of God, or to the will of Satan."[51] And yet, Luther holds that *we* are to blame for sins that we cannot help but commit. We are unable to do what is good—yet we are condemned for our inability! Luther revels in the offensiveness of this doctrine. One scholar summarizes Luther's view thus: "God commands us to do what is impossible in order to goad us and to show us how incapable we are of doing any of the things he commands."[52] If we ask "why He lays this fault to the charge of the will, when man cannot avoid it, it is not lawful to ask."[53] God chooses to save *some* people, but actually *all* deserve damnation, so we cannot complain. Of course, this is deeply offensive to our reason and our sense of fair play, but Luther is happy to say that our reason *needs* to be offended.[54]

The cruelty in Luther's theology reflects the cruel treatment he received as a child and as a young man. His atonement theology seems to arise out of the brutal and abusive upbringing he suffered. Luther had a severe father, and lived in dread of his punishments; his mother also beat him.[55] In his theology, he emphasized the Father's hatred of sin, and the violent punishments he has

---

51. Luther, *The Bondage of the Will* 9, in *Martin Luther*, 188, 190.
52. McSorley, *Luther*, 350.
53. Luther, *The Bondage of the Will* 10, in *Martin Luther*, 192.
54. Ibid., 200.
55. Erikson, *Young Man Luther*, 57–58, 66–67, 123.

prepared for those who "deserve" it—which is everyone! Boiling rage seems to underlie Luther's extreme pessimism about humanity. He believed that a Christian should actually hate himself.[56] He taught that people are wholly corrupt, depraved, and incapable of doing the will of God. Self-loathing is the logical result of such assumptions.

Luther Contrasted with Jesus

Luther's hyper-pessimistic view stands in sharp contrast with Jesus' teaching that people *can* honestly discern and do the will of God: "Anyone who resolves to do the will of God will know whether the teaching is from God or whether I am speaking on my own" (John 7:17). In fact, "whoever does the will of God is my brother and sister and mother" (Mark 3:35). Instead of calling people helpless sinners, Jesus says they can "be children of the Most High," can "be merciful, just as your Father is merciful" (Luke 6:35–36). How is it that so many people have accepted Luther's gloomy view, when Jesus says just the opposite?

The *honest heart* needs to be rediscovered by Christians. For too long, many Christians have accepted Luther's cynicism, his rejection of even the *possibility* of someone being a good person. Luther insists "the just man sins in every good work,"[57] but Jesus says "The good person out of the good treasure of the heart produces good" (Luke 6:45). And in case that isn't clear enough, he says some people will "hear the word, hold it fast in an *honest* and *good* heart, and bear fruit with patient endurance" (Luke 8:15).

How much clearer could it be? We are to receive the word in an honest heart! Jesus is not fantasizing. He is talking about the process of receiving truth and bearing spiritual fruit. This is not the logic of substitutionary death or violent "payment" for sin. Rather, it is the sensible process of people joyously receiving the life and the guidance that their spiritual Parent generously offers.

56. Luther, *Commentary on Romans* 100.9; in Rashdall, *The Idea of the Atonement*, 401.

57. Quoted in Rashdall, *The Idea of the Atonement*, 402.

If Jesus thought that people were totally evil, why would he call himself the "Son of Man," identifying himself with "man"? Why would he say "Blessed are the pure in heart" (Matt 5:8) if he thought *no one* was pure in heart? Jesus shows us the best of what a human being can be, affirming the possibility of *sincere* and *honest* relationship with the heavenly Father. He exhorts us to "hunger and thirst for righteousness" (Matt 5:6). Obviously, then, people really can hunger for what is *right*. This contradicts the notion that people are wholly depraved, a doctrine that leads to religious bullying and the shaming of children. Christianity has been damaged—*people* have been damaged—by the cruel teaching and parenting that results from this shame-based theology. It is time to outgrow the anti-humanitarian attitude that has poisoned Christianity.

Luther's extreme cynicism is simply irreconcilable with Jesus' positive teachings. On this point, believers need to choose between Jesus and Luther. Whom do you believe?

What To Say about Luther

I want to give Luther credit for his honesty about his spiritual struggles. His sincerity gave moral power to his protest against greedy and manipulative church leaders. But his theology was poisoned by his internalizing of the pessimism and cruelty of his abusive parents and teachers. Extreme pessimism was the "logical" conclusion. It is not surprising that a child who was tormented should internalize the abuse, and grow up believing in a cruel God.

Unfortunately, resentment and spite ended up taking over Luther's mind. Early in his writing career, he had repudiated the anti-Semitic blood libel and criticized the preachers who "embitter the hearts of the faithful against" Jews.[58] This was part of his strategy of winning over the Jews. But later in life, when Luther realized that his preaching was not going to convert the Jews, he lashed out at them, writing *On the Jews and Their Lies*. This work repeated

---

58. Carroll, *Constantine's Sword*, 366.

the vicious allegations of Jews poisoning wells and kidnapping children. He called them "the Devil's children."[59] This ugly work of Luther's was centuries later proudly republished and distributed by the Nazis.

Calvin

The most important successor of Luther, and ancestor of the "Reformed" churches, was Jean Calvin of Geneva. Calvin was at least as pessimistic as Luther: "The impurity of parents is transmitted to their children, so that all, without exception, are originally depraved . . . [and] deservedly condemned by God."[60] He repeats Luther's peculiar idea that people "deserve" condemnation, even though they cannot *help* sinning.

Calvin cherished the idea of Jesus dying as a substitute, not only taking on the punishment we deserved, but taking on our actual *guilt*. He was very literal-minded about this, writing, "He took the role of a guilty man and evildoer . . . The guilt that held us liable for punishment has been transferred to the head of the Son of God."[61]

Both Luther and Calvin picture the Father a stern justice-demander, and the Son as a tender mercy-giver. Of course, Jesus never taught such a separation between Father and Son, but stressed his working *together* with the Father. Nor did Paul intend such a severe division between Father and Son, though he *did* open the door to misinterpretation with his metaphors of Jesus' death as a sacrificial offering or a ransom payment.

Luther's and Calvin's theologies develop all the worst possibilities that those metaphors hold. Calvin repeats the doctrine of sinful and guilty babies (*Institutes* 2.1.7–8), and heightens the attack on free will with his doctrine of predestination: everyone is predestined to be either saved or damned; free choice is an illusion.

59. Hsia, *The Myth of Ritual Murder*, 133.

60. Calvin, *Institutes* 2.1.6–7, 1:215, 217.

61. Calvin, *Institutes* 2.16.6; quoted in Dawson, *Flesh Becomes Word*, 50.

Whether one is assigned to be saved or damned is wholly arbitrary and unchangeable. Many Christians rebelled against this thinking at the time it was expressed, and we should rebel against it now.

God is *not*, in fact, tallying up the sins of babies, or even taking such a hostile approach toward adults. Because of God's parental love, salvation is free for the asking—although it has to be genuinely *sincere* asking. Jesus taught that one can go straight to God with faith and honesty, and be saved. There is no court case against all of humanity, no universal guilty verdict, no divine rage that must find a target, no vengeance misdirected against the innocent Son. God is not so unfair, so emotional, or so round-about. James saw this clearly, writing that "there is no variation or shadow" in "the Father of lights," who is the source of "every perfect gift" (Jas 1:17).

The doctrine developed by Calvin is now known as the penal substitutionary theory, because of its notion that Jesus substituted for guilty humanity, became the scapegoat, received the brunt of God's burning anger, and suffered the penalty humans deserved. The pessimism and shame of Augustine and Luther reach their culmination in Calvin's formulation of Jesus' crucifixion as the ultimate ransom payment.

The idea that salvation was purchased goes along with the common idea that there is no free lunch, that everything must be *paid for*. This is materialistic. It projects onto God what are really *human* rules and *material* experiences. It makes false assumptions about the spiritual life. It goes against the idea that God can really *forgive*, can offer salvation without any condemnation, and without any kind of payment. But Jesus taught that God is actually forgiving, and needs no victim to pay for the sins of others. Calvin took Paul's and Hebrews' metaphors too literally and mechanistically. Rachel Held Evans wryly commented that the idea that "'Jesus came to die' . . . reduces the gospel to a transaction, whereby . . . Jesus basically shows up to post our bail."[62]

Why does Christian thinking continue to overlook Jesus' own emphasis, and choose instead these transactional ideas of

62. Evans, *Inspired*, 154.

atonement? Worldly thinking is being projected onto the spiritual level. It is a bad mental habit. It conceals the truth of the love of the Father and his Son. It assumes that there is a huge barrier between us and God, and that God is hostile to us.

The materialistic mind lends itself to simplistic slogans and formulas, which are harmful and distressing when taught to young Christians. The great nineteenth-century Congregationalist Horace Bushnell warns us: "The very idea of preaching Christ by formula, even if the true formula were developed, is a great mistake"; it allows sterile words to crowd out "all the ten thousand flaming truths." What is needed is not a *formula*, but "Christ discovered by the heart, and verified by a deep working Christian experience."[63] Bushnell says it is "akin to superstition" to think that what is needed is "the placation of God by a contribution of the necessary evils," the evils of various punishments.[64] I think it really *is* superstition, not just *akin* to it. Instead of letting fear infect our faith, let us walk humbly with our God, and be not afraid.

Among the "ten thousand flaming truths" that we will discover, some of the important ones are in the area of psychology.

---

63. Bushnell, *The Vicarious Sacrifice*, 527.
64. Ibid., 502.

5

PSYCHOLOGICAL PROBLEMS
WITH ATONEMENT

THE PROBLEM WITH PRIMITIVISM

The worst problem with sacrificial atonement is that it revives primitive religious instincts. The sacrificial metaphor has taken on a life of its own, far beyond what the Bible or the early theologians intended. Its effect in the realm of popular religion is alarming.

Popular atonement concepts have presented a monstrous and primitive God the Father, and a kindly and self-sacrificing God the Son. This rupture is not real, and it is not biblical.

Often, when people take the sacrificial metaphor very literally, they feel they have to defend and promote all the ancient beliefs about sacrifice, such as the notion that a sacrificial death soothes and conciliates God's anger. This is a non-moral idea. It means that God can be manipulated by material means, something the prophets attacked vigorously. Non-moral atonement beliefs take two basic forms: the *magical* concept (that God can be manipulated by ritual practices), and the *propitiatory* concept (that God can be appeased or placated by a sufficient payment or punishment).

Let us look at the magical concept first. This kind of thinking often speaks of "the power of the blood," including the notion that "innocent blood" has cleansing power. This draws from three NT passages: "you were ransomed . . . with the precious blood of Christ, like that of a lamb without defect" (1 Pet 1:18–19); "the blood of Jesus his Son cleanses us from all sin" (1 John 1:7); and "how much more will the blood of Christ . . . purify our conscience" (Heb 9:14). These assume a strange kind of causation, where a *ritual* cause has a *moral* effect. Instead, a moral effect should require a *moral* cause.

The propitiatory concept is perhaps more logical (*rigidly* logical) than the magical concept. Propitiation is crudely *economic*: conceiving of a certain legal tender *purchasing* salvation. That legal tender was the Savior's *innocent suffering*. This glorifies suffering, and falls into a psychological trap that generates guilt and anxiety, and *expects* or even *justifies* the inflicting of suffering upon the innocent. It is "for your own good."[1] Calvin was particularly fond of expressing the payment concept: "If the effect of his shed blood is, that our sins are not imputed to us, it follows, that by that price the justice of God was satisfied . . . [by] the payment or compensation which acquits us from guilt."[2] Even righteousness is purchased: "by paying what others owed, he might acquire righteousness for them."[3]

The manipulative psychology of blood atonement keeps Christianity chained to some of the most primitive ways of thinking. It projects human sacrificial thinking onto God. People end up believing that God really is *paid off* by a ritual murder! Of course, Christian apologists do not use the phrase "paid off," and certainly not "ritual murder." Nor would they knowingly defend the concept of manipulating God, but that is exactly what they are *unconsciously* promoting. With Luther and Calvin, however, it was fully conscious. They had no problem saying that salvation was

1. The title of a groundbreaking book that explored the psychological effects of parental bullying and terrorizing of children: Miller, *For Your Own Good.*

2. Calvin, *Institutes* 2.17.4, 5, 1:456–57.

3. Calvin, *Institutes* 2.17.4, 1:456.

purchased by a ransom payment to God. But nowadays people feel a need to downplay or even deny the manipulation that this entails.

In fact, scratch the surface of most popular atonement teachings, and you discover either the magical or the propitiatory concept, or both. Christian apologists should *notice* the manipulative logic that their arguments imply, and should ask whether this logic fits with what Jesus taught. People should stop sweeping under the rug the problems that atonement teachings carry.

The message of salvation needs to be separated from all superstitious ideas, including the idea of using sacrifice to either cleanse impurity or appease God's anger. Jesus was pronouncing people saved without any reference to his coming death. His life, his ministry, his acts of kindness *mattered*; they were not a pointless prelude to the only thing that mattered (his death). Even *after* that barbaric act of judicial murder, God and Jesus were saving people *in spite of* the crucifixion. We need to stop blaming God for that act of human evil!

Salvation is not a magical cleansing or a sacrificial payment made on our behalf. There is no magical power in blood. Wrongdoing, of course, *does* carry personal and social consequences, and these must be addressed. There are *actual* sins committed by *particular* people, and these need to be adjudicated fairly (possibly restricting a person's freedom). A Christian who has sinned needs to repent and to make reparation, as well as make a decision and determination that the sins will not be repeated. This takes the courage of one's convictions. And all of this is a moral and social process, not a magical one. Preachers should stop saying "we are all sinners, but his blood covers our sin." This is a magical solution, and it evades personal responsibility. It's a recipe for further sinning, and half-hearted apologies after getting caught.

If you have committed sin, then *admit* it wholeheartedly. Change your life, reform your habits, and make reparations to people whom you have hurt. Admission of sin does not involve a magical escape from the consequences of sin. Be a *responsible* repenter, like Zacchaeus the tax-collector who said he would give back, with interest, any money he had extorted (Luke 19:8).

There is no sin that can be paid for by a ritual killing. Such an atrocious teaching is inconsistent with the spiritual character of the Father of whom Jesus taught. God does not need sacrifice, payment, or revenge. Nor does God oppress humanity with unbearable guilt or heavy ritual requirements. "If you had known what this means, 'I desire mercy and not sacrifice,' you would not have condemned the guiltless" (Matt 12:7).

PSYCHOLOGICAL UNDERCURRENTS

Sacrifice has troubling psychological undercurrents, especially when it is blended with "satisfaction," which implies appeasing God's anger. This kind of theology assumes that God is a strict boss who is keeping track of who's "naughty and nice," and preparing the worst possible punishments for the naughty ones. This is not the real God, but is a projection of human assumptions about how a strict father or king would rule. God is not an insecure monarch who needs repeated demonstrations of submission and suffering from his subjects.

Most theologians try to do better than that, of course. Atonement theology usually joins primitive religious instincts with a teaching about God as a loving Father. The surface of atonement theology involves the love of God, but the underlying reality is that of needing to soothe and placate an angry God. It may be that this derives from the learned behavior of coping with parental rage.

I believe that some atonement ideas have a background in dysfunctional family history. Ransom and penitential suffering are religious echoes of a childhood strategy for coping with parental brutality by *payment through suffering*. An oppressive home life, wherein the children must appease parental anger by being *seen to suffer*, contributes to the paranoid underpinning of the atonement concept. Children learn to placate their angry parents by paying for their sins, while in atonement theology an angry parental God is appeased by seeing someone suffer for humanity's sins. This kind of theology arises from authoritarian parenting. Harsh theology gets handed on down through the generations, just as patterns of abuse get handed on from generation to generation.

Even though atonement advocates claim that the price was paid once and for all, their rhetoric shows that they assume that debts must *continue* to be paid, as though the heavenly Father is *still* angry, and needs to punish someone. In some families, there is a pattern of scapegoating the most artistic or sensitive child.[4] One of the children is designated the "black sheep," the blame-taker. It can be the most religious or conscientious child who is ostracized, bullied, and targeted. Even among adults, a person who takes relationships and ethics seriously may be the one who is slandered and attacked, even by Christians. Many Christians are wholly worldly, and unaware of how distant they are, in spirit and in truth, from Jesus.

It is true: "People who refuse to face their faults find scapegoats; those who know their own weaknesses, do not seem to need scapegoats."[5] People with primitive religious beliefs often unconsciously construct abusive environments in their homes and churches, in which scapegoats are selected and punished, and violence is justified. The abusive pattern at the heart of their theology gets re-enacted in their personal lives.

We need to break free of such distortion, even if it requires decades of therapy and relearning how to love without manipulation. The notion of *paying off* God is terrible and immoral. It re-enacts a pathological family pattern of fear and punishment. Distorted human behaviors and patterns are being projected onto God.

Only if God were abusive would it make sense to approach the Deity with groveling and displays of suffering. But Jesus taught that the Father is loving and forgiving, just as *he* (Jesus) is. We must stop assuming that God is cruel or violent, or that God is a tyrant who demands absolute obedience.

As Rebecca Ann Parker wrote, "Do we really believe that God is appeased by cruelty, and wants nothing more than our

4. Bermann, *Scapegoat*, 181–82.

5. Allport and Postman, *The Psychology of Rumor*, 42.

obedience? . . . If God is imagined as a fatherly torturer, earthly parents are also justified, perhaps even required, to teach through violence."[6] But this idea is abhorrent. Parker objects to all theologies of "mystified violence."[7] "The spiritualizing of suffering makes God the author of all pain, who uses pain to edify or purify human beings."[8] This is a falsehood that teaches people that they should endure abuse.

Although doctrines of substitutionary atonement are common in families where harsh parenting occurs, not all conservative parents are harsh toward their children. Many conservative parents treat their parental duties as a sacred honor, characterized by love. This acceptance of responsibility enables sincerity and love to triumph over doctrine.

Nevertheless, there tends to be a correlation between religious conservatism (whether Jewish, Muslim, Hindu, or Christian) and harsh or abusive parenting. There is a connection between cruel parental control and rigid religious conservatism. The idea of God as harsh or violent only "rings true" for those who encountered violence in their homes, who learned that they must be *seen to suffer* so as to avoid even worse punishment. It is true "that many religious ideas that children are taught cause them emotional torment" through "shaming" and suppression of the child's feelings.[9]

SHAME AND FUNDAMENTALISM

I have already begun to move away from mere *ideas* that are harmful, and to discuss the *emotions* and experiences that people have endured, in their search for truth. For people who have lived through a fundamentalist phase in their faith, the overwhelming and crippling experience they have endured is *shame*. Shame is the experience of being unlovable, damaged, bad, unwanted, or

6. Parker, from Brock and Parker, *Proverbs of Ashes*, 30–31.

7. Ibid., 48.

8. Ibid., 44.

9. Capps, *The Child's Song*, 51–53.

worthless at one's core. Thus, it can be deeper and more painful than *guilt*, which is the consciousness of having *done* something wrong. Shame is the feeling of *being* something wrong, of being ridiculous, ugly, weak, or disgusting. Chronic shame is debilitating. It leads to depression, self-loathing, abject sorrow or feelings of emptiness, and it may result in acts of self-harm.[10] Guilt might motivate one to make changes in one's life, but shame leaves one hopeless and immobilized. Guilt can speak its sorrow, and act on its remorse. Shame paralyzes and renders a person helpless.

Shame is a common experience that survivors of fundamentalism (or any kind of abusive system) have had. My definition of "fundamentalism" is any ideology that insists on the perfection of its Scriptures; demands conformity of belief and behavior; and promises reward for those who conform, and punishment for those who do not. This definition is broad enough that it allows for Islamic fundamentalists, Hindu fundamentalists, Catholic fundamentalists, and those to whom the term is most *usually* applied—Protestant fundamentalists. Often there is a simple summary of belief (such as "Jesus purchased us from burning in hell") that will be uttered as though it were a perfectly accurate summation and not, in fact, an over-simplification and a *distortion* of the Scriptures. The Bible is much more diverse and open-ended than that. There is such a rich banquet of teachings in the Bible—what a travesty, to dumb it down to a simplistic slogan based on a few atonement passages! Think of the many salvation teachings that have nothing to do with atonement, such as "Love your enemies and pray for those who persecute you, so that you may be children of your Father in heaven" (Matt 5:44–45); "anyone who gives you a cup of water in my name because you belong to the Messiah will certainly not lose their reward" (Mark 9:41 NIV); "if you confess with your lips that Jesus is Lord and believe in your heart that God raised him from the dead, you will be saved" (Rom 10:9).

Many survivors of fundamentalism describe intense social pressure, indoctrination, experiences of shaming, and teachings of a harsh and judgmental God. Doug Frank wrote a book about the

10. Pattison, "Shame and the Unwanted Self," 12–16.

debate about God among Protestant evangelicals. He says "Many evangelicals—who 'know' theoretically that God is infinitely loving—feel secretly oppressed by the 'majestic,' powerful, harsh and condemning 'Father' who lived in Luther's heart."[11] The term *evangelical* is not restricted to fundamentalists. It includes many who reject fundamentalism (including some who were *formerly* a part of it). Many of those who have departed from fundamentalism tell stories of their fathers being distant, or being stern disciplinarians. "Such stories suggest that the natural urge to overcome shame—shame inflicted in childhood and reinforced by their association with fundamentalism—helps explain the attraction of many evangelical scholars to an abstract and distant God, a surrogate 'Father' whose sovereignty camouflages an incapacity for warm connection."[12] Even the title of the chapter from which I draw this quote is revealing: "The God that Shame Built: Yearning for a respectable father."[13]

If God is remote and angry, then "we are certainly not saved from the voice inside us that hates us."[14] Many people carry that internal voice with them their whole lives, even when they believe they have been saved from their "deserved" fate. When children are taught this pessimistic doctrine, the psychological effects can be life-long. But Frank asks, "Wouldn't a loving God wish to lighten our burden of guilt?"[15] Of course! Salvation, then, would address the underlying problem of shame.

Fear-dominated religious ideas do real harm to people, especially to children. The hurtful influence goes in the other direction, as well: a dysfunctional family tends to make people vulnerable to bad theology. I have been digging for the psychological roots of the punishing God idea, and I have come upon the writings of a now-neglected pioneer in the field of psychoanalysis, who sheds some light on this. I present his theory here.

11. Frank, *A Gentler God*, 197–98.

12. Ibid., 95–96.

13. Ibid., 59.

14. Ibid., 126.

15. Ibid.

ATONEMENT AS MANIPULATIVE SUFFERING

Sandor Rado was a psychologist who studied under Freud but went his own way and tried to develop a more well-balanced theory of psychology, moving away from the "libido theory" and its over-emphasis on instinct, focusing instead on how people adapt, learn, and cope.[16] Rado had some keen insights about atonement as a psychological strategy. He spoke of the child enduring some estrangement or anger from the parents, and of atonement being the child's attempt to *appease* parental anger and win back that love. Encountering parental anger, the child is frightened, and seeks to soothe or accommodate the parent. The child internalizes the parental rage and finds a solution to that rage.

> He begins *unconsciously* to reproduce within his mind the punishments anticipated from his parents and, in doing so, he unconsciously *hopes to win love* . . . Self-punishment takes place in the hope of absolution and has its origin in the longing for love . . . [There is a] close connection between *guilt, atonement* and *forgiveness*.[17]

The sequence seems to be like this: the child experiences parental anger and punishment; the child learns that the punishment is followed by restoration of parental love; the child learns to undergo suffering in order to win back the love. The child even learns to *initiate* the suffering: to engage in self-punishment. This pattern, learned in childhood, continues in adulthood. Rado argues that depression is the adult manifestation of self-punishment as a self-protective strategy. One could call it a desperate quest for reconciliation and approval:

> Depression is a desperate cry for love, precipitated by a serious loss . . . The emotional overreaction to this emergency unfolds as an expiatory process of self-punishment . . . undertaken with the unconscious intent of reconciling the mother.[18]

16. Ovesy, "Introduction to Part I," 9.
17. Rado, "The Problem of Melancholia," 1:51.
18. Rado, "The Border Region," 1:326.

"Expiatory" here means removing the guilt and alienation. Of course, self-punishment seems like an extreme choice, but its purpose is very sensible: regaining parental approval. The child is internalizing the pattern of punishment and forgiveness it has learned. Its behavior can become completely unconscious, and this person as an adult may not understand his own self-punishing behavior.

> Parental reproach gives rise to self-reproach, parental punishment to self-punishment, parental forgiveness to self-forgiveness. In the course of time, this expiatory procedure can become completely automatic: the child, and later the adult, executes the pattern without having the remotest inkling of what he is doing.[19]

The behavior can become extreme because the emotions are so intense. The child will undergo whatever is necessary "to propitiate his parents and be again loved and cared for . . . [T]he severity of self-punishment . . . may far exceed the severity of parental punishment. We face here the action of a force stronger and more compelling than fear."[20] The need for love and approval is the force stronger than fear.

I am giving so much space to Rado's thinking because I think he has correctly identified one of the emotional/psychological roots of atonement thinking, even though his focus is not on religion. I think Rado has correctly identified the fear, guilt, frustration, and manipulation that form the powerful emotional ancestry of atonement. Indeed, in all the religions we can see self-punishing or self-shaming behaviors designed to achieve holiness or reconciliation. Many religious practices involve suffering. Fasting, for instance, is a "form of expiatory self-punishment. 'You need not punish me, I am doing it myself.'"[21]

Self-punishment in religion is an attempt to manipulate God, to impress God through one's penances. I use the words

19. Rado, "Rage, Violence, and Conscience," 2:148.

20. Rado, "The Automatic Motivating System," 2:168.

21. Ibid., 2:171.

manipulate and *manipulative*; Rado prefers the word *coercive*,[22] but they signify the same thing: the assumption that the parent or the parental God had to be *persuaded* to be kindly. Atonement, even Christian atonement, is fundamentally manipulative, whether in the suffering and penance that some believers undertake, or in the theology that sees Christ's suffering as a *price* paid to obtain forgiveness, as Calvin argued: "He by his death purchased life for us."[23] This is based on the mistaken belief that Christ's death somehow appeased God's wrath.

Sandor Rado placed his finger upon the psychological key to atonement and depression. The pattern of guilt-atonement-forgiveness he observed occurs in many religions, but it is a particular focus in some Christian theology. Not all Christians who use the term *atonement* mean the same thing, but many of them perpetuate the largely Calvinist theology in which guilt, shame, and punishment are projected onto the scapegoat, Christ, who drained away the Father's presumed wrath, and persuaded the Father to forgive.

It is all an attempt to manipulate God, but it is unnecessary. God actually *desires* to give the salvation that is so anxiously sought: "Do not be afraid, little flock, for it is your Father's good pleasure to give you the kingdom" (Luke 12:32). We need to hear the generous *tone* of this saying, as well as its content. God does not need to be persuaded to offer salvation or love. Unfortunately, if we have learned fear from an early age, we will have difficulty wrapping our minds around the idea of a truly loving parent who requires no atonement, but actually responds to sincere repentance. Jeremiah taught that God is *eager* to reach us, and even helps us to be responsive: "I will put my law within them, and I will write it on their hearts . . . I will forgive their iniquity, and remember their sin no more" (Jer 31:33–34).

Some ardent believers have made deeply personal statements about the love Jesus has for his followers, and they speak of his death as a selfless and saving act on his part. Of course, they are

22. Ibid., 2:170–71.
23. Calvin, *Institutes* 2.16.7, 1:440.

correct about his heroic action, and there is no denying the authentic faith experience that these believers are having, nor will I challenge their certainty that Jesus saves them. I *do* want to warn them about the psychological damage that is caused by teaching that God *required* the Son's death. I *do* worry about the difficulties they are creating for new Christians by imposing the logic of substitutionary suffering and death upon trusting minds.

Many believers seem to be helpless victims of atonement ideology and its accompanying threat of hell. Much could be said about the psychological force of the traditional (really, medieval) teaching on hell. This would be a good place to take a glance at the origin of the Christian concept of hell.

THE ORIGIN OF HELL

The older English translations give the word *hell* for the Greek word *gehenna*. Newer translations tend not to use that word. I think that where the Gospels have Jesus speaking of *gehenna* (or *ge-hinnom* in Hebrew), it ought to be translated "judgment" or "condemnation"[24] rather than "hell." *Ge-hinnom/gehenna* was the name of a valley on the south side of Jerusalem where people threw garbage, including the corpses of criminals and others.[25] The place aroused disgust at its mere mention. Maggots were said always to be growing in the refuse there, and a fire (mainly to burn the corpses) was perpetually smoldering. This is probably what is referred to at the end of Isaiah, although the author does not use the term *gehenna*, in speaking of "those who rebelled against me; their worm will not die, nor will their fire be quenched" (Isa 66:24).[26]

It was also the place where forbidden pagan rituals were practiced (Jer 7:31–32; 19:2–11). The historical authors mention kings who participated in these "abominable practices of the nations," such as King Ahaz, who "made his sons pass through fire" in this

24. Also: Jersak, *Her Gates Will Never Be Shut*, 39, 61.

25. Baker, *Razing Hell*, 129.

26. Ibid., 129–30.

valley (2 Chron 28:3; 2 Kings 16:3 has "son," and does not mention the valley), and King Menasseh, who did the same with his son (2 Kings 21:6; 2 Chr 33:6). Evidently, improper rituals were continuing in Jeremiah's time; the prophet threatens the partakers in these rituals with death in that valley, which would be renamed "the Valley of Slaughter . . . I will give their dead bodies for food to the birds of the air" (Jer 19:6–7). It is *this-worldly* punishment that is promised. *Gehenna* "is not associated with hell or afterlife in the Hebrew Bible."[27] The prophetic threats related to *gehenna* are connected with the fate of Jerusalem, and this is how a number of scholars understand the *gehenna* references in the Jesus tradition, for instance: "All of Jesus' references to Gehenna . . . are actually about the coming judgment on Israel."[28]

In the intertestamental period, ideas of punishment were expanded, including the idea of fiery punishment in the afterlife, possibly drawing upon the beliefs of Zoroastrianism, the great Persian religion that put an emphasis on judgment and afterlife. An existing Jewish idea such the "'day of the Lord' . . . develops quickly into apocalypticism under the influence of Persian thought."[29] The collection of works now called *1 Enoch*, written in the three centuries before Jesus, contains scenes of a fiery afterlife judgment of rebel angels and human sinners (*1 Enoch* 7:36; 48:9–10; 54:1–2; 90:24–26).[30] These ideas were accepted by many Jews, and then by Christians, finding their way into the New Testament, specifically in Mark and Matthew. Using the language of Isaiah 66:24, Mark describes *gehenna* as the place "where their worm never dies, and the fire is never quenched" (Mark 9:47–48). But this passage got corrupted at an early date; the Isaian phrase was inserted at two places slightly earlier, which became verses 44 and 46 in later manuscripts. The marginal notes to the NRSV say that "Verses 44 and 46 . . . are lacking in the best ancient authorities," that is, the oldest and most reliable manuscripts. I think they were lacking

27. Segal, *Life After Death*, 135.
28. Ansell, "Hell," 201.
29. Segal, *Life After Death*, 183; see also Baker, *Razing Hell*, 128.
30. Jersak, *Her Gates Will Never Be Shut*, 44–45.

in Jesus' teachings, as well. I can accept that Jesus uttered a threat about "judgment" or "condemnation," but not these apocalyptic teachings about fire and damnation.

Matthew is clearly more attached to the hell idea than Mark is; he speaks of the "unquenchable fire" (3:12) and the *gehenna of fire*" (18:9). Matthew would have loved this Isaian line about worms and fire if it had been present in the original version of Mark. But, in fact, this is one of the few lines from Mark that Matthew does *not* incorporate. Nor does Luke include the undying worms and fire. Maybe it was not present in the original version of Mark. The considerable alteration in the manuscript tradition of Mark 9 throws doubt on the whole passage.

In any case, there was considerable debate and disagreement about what *gehenna* meant in the time of Jesus, from the prophetic concept of the judgment of Jerusalem, to the idea of an infernal place of prolonged punishment, but, Jersak argues, "Jesus' Gehenna was rooted in Jeremiah's prophetic-historic tradition rather than the infernalist underworld."[31] Ansell agrees with Jersak's (and my) assessment that the historical Jesus held to Jeremiah's view ("judgment of Jerusalem") rather than to the hell-fire concept: "The Gehenna of the Gospels, I suggest, continues the OT tradition of imminent, this-worldly judgment."[32]

The harsh doctrine of hell inflicts fear and guilt upon believers, in contrast to Jesus' own teaching to "fear not" (Matt 10:31; Luke 12:7, 32). The very literal and sadistically spelled-out concept of hell is mostly a product of the Christian Dark Ages. The supposed cruelty of God was really an echo of the cruelty of medieval punishments. I would like to toss the hell doctrine into the nearest abyss, and return to Jesus' own teachings—and in *this* case, to Paul's teachings, as well. Paul did not teach damnation. He clearly says "the wages of sin are death" (Rom 6:23). Sinners "perish" (Rom 2:12; 2 Cor 4:3). Eternal life is contrasted with death (Rom 5:21). Fleshly living reaps corruption; spiritual living reaps eternal life (Gal 6:8).

31. Ibid., 51n60.
32. Ansell, "Hell," 200.

The hell concept is part of the effort to frighten and push people into faith, in sharp contrast to the appeal to love and decency[33] that characterized the teachings of Jesus: his appeal to the innocence of children, his image of bearing good fruit.[34] My goal is to throw a life-line to those who sense that they are being swamped by harmful theology, and who wish they could attain a better understanding of what Jesus *really* taught, and what God *really* offers.

Divine love conquers all. This needs to be remembered not only about Jesus but about the *Father*. The problem with most atonement teachings is not what they say about *Jesus* (the Merciful Son), but what they say about the *Father* (that he is a sacrifice-demander). Jesus insisted that "your Father is merciful" (Luke 6:36); "the Father himself loves you" (John 16:27). It does no good to believe that the Son is merciful, if one thinks that the Father is sadistic and vengeful. One could hardly trust the "love" that would come from such a Deity.

---

33. I refer to the many teachings that appeal to honesty, kindness, and humility (Matt 5:3–9; 7:1–5; 23:12; Mark 12:44; Luke 16:10–13; 18:9–14). Not just "faith," but *character* matters.

34. Matt 5:17; 18:4; Mark 4:20, 26–28; Luke 18:15–17.

6

WHAT OF CHRISTOLOGY?

CREATOR POWER

What, then, happens to Christology, if we reject the idea that salvation was purchased for sinful mankind by the death of Jesus as a substitute? I think we are forced to return to the *original* basis for Christology: Jesus' divinity and his role in creation. "In the beginning was the Word . . . All things came into being through (διά [*dia*]) him, and without him not one thing came into being" (John 1:1, 3). He is the creator!

Christology needs to be founded not on *what was done to Jesus*, but upon *who Jesus is*. The early Greek Fathers *knew* this. Surely Jesus' role as creator or co-creator of the earth itself is a far more legitimate basis for Christology than any magical thinking about the violence done to him. If we base Christology on an atrocity, or upon an *interpretation* of the atrocity, then we have allowed the murderers to set the agenda. No atrocity is ever approved by God, or required by God. All the shameful acts of injustice and murder that people commit are signs of *human* barbarity. We need to grow up morally and repudiate all barbarism, including in our religious thinking.

Let us look at that often-neglected teaching that Jesus was the creator or co-creator. There are four passages from four different parts of the New Testament (Gospels, Pauline letters, Deutero-Pauline letters, and Catholic Epistles) that say this. Similarly to John, Hebrews says that God, through Jesus, created the worlds: "through (διά [*dia*]) whom he also created the worlds" (Heb 1:2). The "he" in this passage refers to God, the "whom" is Jesus. Jesus is the creative agent *through* whom God created. Actually, the words translated "the worlds" here are "the eons" (τοὺς αἰῶνας [*tous aiōnas*]). So Jesus is the co-creator of the eons! "Worlds" is probably the best translation here, though it could also mean "the ages."

The other three passages clearly refer to Jesus creating (or co-creating) "all things." In Colossians we read: "He is the image of the invisible God . . . [I]n (ἐν [*en*]) him all things in heaven and on earth were created" (Col 1:15–16). So all things were created *in* him. There is more to say about the Colossians passage, but first I want to trace this idea of creation *in* or *through* Jesus, since it appears in 1 Corinthians 8:6. Here, Paul insists both upon monotheism and upon Jesus' partnership with God: "for us there is one God, the Father, from whom are all things and for whom we exist, and one Lord, Jesus Christ, through (διά [*dia*]) whom are all things and through whom we exist." Once again, there is creation "through" Jesus, and we see the same preposition in John 1:3 and Hebrews 1:2.

I have used the term "co-creator," but I am not insisting on "co-creator" over "creator." Either term will do, as long as we recognize that the New Testament teaches that Jesus was the creator or co-creator of the world and of the human race! This is too important a teaching to neglect or downplay. It is because of *who Jesus is* that he is the Savior. Who he is . . . is the co-creator of this world.

In the early church, this was more widely recognized and preached on than it has been in recent centuries. Jesus as *creator* needs to be recovered. Jesus had creator power before he ever came to earth, so it is no surprise that he had Savior power when he came to earth. His Savior power was always inherent in him. It did not arise when he was scapegoated.

Hebrews says he created "the worlds" or "eons," and the other three passages say he created "all things" (τὰ πάντα [*ta panta*];

Colossians 1:16–18 uses that phrase four times). The Colossians passage may be the most explicit. Here I give it in full: "In him all things in heaven and on earth were created, things visible and invisible, whether thrones or dominions or rulers or powers—all things have been created through him and for him. He himself is before all things, and in him all things hold together" (Col 1:16–17). The "thrones," "dominions," and "rulers" most likely refer to the heavenly or angelic powers.[1] Of more immediate interest to us is that "all things" includes the human race.

To give the full picture, we have to stress not only Jesus' divine creative role, but his incarnating as a human being. One of the best passages to spell out the dual nature of Jesus is the second chapter of the Epistle to the Hebrews. As Son of Man, he is our elder brother ("Jesus is not ashamed to call them brothers"; regarding the "flesh and blood" that we inhabit, "he himself likewise shared the same things," Heb 2:11, 14); as Son of God and creator of worlds, he is our creator-father ("Here am I and the children whom God has given me," 2:13). Our creator humbled himself and incarnated as a fellow human. He is not aloof from human suffering, since he experienced suffering as a human being, and not only in the crucifixion, but throughout his life, enduring the incomprehension of his family (Mark 3:21), the dull-wittedness of his disciples (Matt 6:30), and the hard-heartedness of the religious leaders.

It is important to know that our creator understands our sufferings. "He had to become like his brothers and sisters in every respect" (Heb 2:17). As Son of God, Jesus reveals the nature of God. As Son of Man, he reveals what a man can be. And as having this dual nature, he reveals that God has compassion on human beings. This shows the richness of Creator Christology.

Now, is any of this threatened by the scientific viewpoint? Absolutely not. There is no necessary contradiction between the biblical concept of a creator and the scientific concept of evolution. Rather, evolution adds another dimension, a cosmic dimension, to Christology. We can think of Jesus as the creative power who set

---

1. Lightfoot, *Saint Paul's Epistles to the Colossians*, 150–51.

the stars awhirl, who designed biological life, and put evolution in motion. Evolution does not contradict creation; rather, evolution is *slow* creation. A number of philosophers have understood Jesus to be working through the created order. Putting evolution and theology into conversation with each other has yielded many fruitful results, from the nineteenth-century thinker who argued that "The individual man is partly the animal from which he has come, and partly the God who is coming into him,"[2] to twenty-first century titles on the topic by a theologian[3] and a biology professor.[4]

In creation, Jesus acts *with* and *for* God. In his earth life, he did the same. In sum, Jesus is *God-in-time*, embodying the divine creativity in the realm of time and space. What is this "power that also enables him to make all things subject to himself" (Phil 3:21), and why does it take so long for this to be accomplished? It seems obvious that Jesus has not yet exerted full control over this material realm he has created. He has to struggle, he has to contend with all the obstacles the material level can present. Evolution is a form of divine creativity that takes epochs to develop and mature. The imperfection of the world, the evil of humanity, do not negate the reality of the perfect and complete God-in-eternity, they only suggest that God-in-time is an unfinished project. We have always known that it is difficult to reconcile perfection in eternity with the frank reality of imperfection in time and space. Adding the scientific dimension deepens the complexity of the problem, but also provides a partial answer to our questions about the presence of suffering, delays, and imperfection.

The human race is a long project that Jesus has undertaken, but he did not create us in vain. Eventually, Jesus "hands over the kingdom to God the Father . . . so that God may be all in all" (1 Cor 15:24, 28). There will come a day when the mentality and spirituality of Christ will permeate the human race, will even conquer sin and violence, and will bring the will of God into manifestation. God is working on the garden: "as the earth brings forth its shoots,

2. Abbott, *The Evolution of Christianity*, 255.

3. Savary, *Teilhard de Chardin*—The Divine Milieu *Explained*.

4. Falk, *Coming to Peace with Science*.

and as a garden causes what is sown in it to spring up, so the LORD God will cause righteousness and praise to spring up before all the nations" (Isa 61:11). This is a crucial biblical promise, although pastors rarely refer to it nowadays. The day will come, when "the earth will be full of the knowledge of the LORD as the waters cover the sea" (Isa 11:9). These prophecies *matter*. They were part of the Jewish hope, and of Jesus' *own* hope when he was a young man. He quotes from both of these just-cited chapters; he uses Isaiah 61 to announce what his own ministry will be like ("recovery of sight to the blind," Luke 4:18), and he cites Isaiah 11:3–4 when he says "Do not judge by appearances, but judge with right judgment" (John 7:24).

The message of Jesus has been sown in the soil of humanity. When it is joined with the insights of science, we have the two elements that work toward the elimination of superstition and ignorance. We still have a long journey ahead of us. Will we learn to harvest the benefits of spiritual progress and scientific understanding? Will we learn to be better parents, better citizens, and better stewards of the earth?

It should be obvious that science does not destroy Christology. In fact, it opens up new possibilities for connecting Christology to philosophy and anthropology. Passages that speak of transformation start to take on a fuller meaning. We have already looked at that amazing statement of Paul's, that believers will be transformed, degree by degree, into the Lord's image, that is, Jesus' image (2 Cor 3:18). The character of Jesus is not only our *guide* for spiritual growth, but is the actual *goal* of our growth. Growing towards God means, more concretely, growing toward Jesus: we will "be conformed to the image of his Son" (Rom 8:29). Using the language of "glory" to speak of spiritual change, Paul says "those whom he justified he also glorified" (Rom 8:30).

John affirms this principle in his epistle: "Beloved, we are God's children now; what we will be has not yet been revealed. What we do know is this: when he is revealed, we will be like him, for we will see him as he is" (1 John 3:2). What more could any Christian ask for than to "be like him," more and more?

As I mentioned in connection with the Greek Fathers, this concept of spiritual transformation toward the image of Christ has a name; it is called *theōsis. Theōsis* is Godward growth, everlasting life, and transformation. *Theōsis* is to some degree a neglected theme in Western Christianity, but it is being rediscovered by many.[5]

It is quite logical for there to be stages in our spiritual growth, just as there are stages of growth in our *earth* life. Jesus says "In my Father's house are many mansions . . . I go to prepare a place for you" (John 14:2–3). He reassures people that they will have a secure home, a place to live and grow. The purpose of the afterlife is abundant living and learning and loving—really the same as the purpose of *this* life.

When these teachings are understood, it is obvious that we are not saved because of an arbitrary decision by God to save a *few*. Rather, we are saved because our spiritual parent, Jesus, loves us as a father, and takes an interest in our growth. Life here on earth is often not fair, and not everyone gets a fair chance to succeed. But everyone *will* get a fair chance to choose eternal life. Jesus says "anyone who comes to me I will never drive away" (John 6:37). He welcomes "all you that are weary" (Matt 11:28). "Let anyone who is thirsty come to me" (John 7:37).

HEALING POWER

This connecting of Christology to Jesus' creatorship is actually the recovery of the original foundation of Christology. It is the *life-giver* who saves us, who nurtures us, as a loving parent. The giving of salvation turns out to be no different than a parent's giving of care. The parent is eager to help. When we see how Jesus responded to a person who reached out to him, we are witnessing the response of a loving parent to a needy child. We receive salvation from Jesus like the woman received healing when she reached out for the hem of his garment, and Jesus said, "I noticed that power had gone out

5. See, for instance, Russell, *The Doctrine of Deification*; and Finlan and Kharlamov, eds., *Theōsis*.

from me" (Luke 8:46). Eternal life comes out from the one who gave us life in the *first* place. He gives life *now*, just as he gave life and healing to those who called on him when he walked this earth. The Son has "life in himself" (John 5:26).

If Jesus is the creator, it should not be at all surprising that he has the power of healing. Someone who has the power to *create life* may logically have the power to *repair* it. Faith opens up a connection to the creative power—the source of healing as well as salvation. "What do you want me to do for you?" Jesus asks (Luke 18:41), and the request for healing is understood as a request for salvation, so besides performing the healing, he says "your faith has saved you" (18:42). Jesus is responsive to human need, but we have to be honest about our need. We have to *know* that we need help. Jesus makes this point when he defends a woman who is being criticized by some arrogant Pharisees. He says "Those who are well have no need of a physician, but those who are sick. Go and learn what this means, 'I desire mercy, not sacrifice.' For I have come to call not the righteous but sinners" (Matt 9:12–13). This is not directed against those who have righteous qualities, but against those who are *self-righteous*, and who think they need no help. He can only help those who *know* they need help.

The healings cease to be so extraordinary and strange if we recognize them as the natural response of a divine parent to the need of a child. It is true that the responses then were more sudden and thoroughgoing than the slow and partial responses that *our* prayers usually receive here and now. Jesus will eventually respond to us as thoroughly as he did to all the needy people who called out to him. Only, we have to put up with a time delay, which was not the case (for some needy people) when the Incarnated Son was physically present on earth. The time delay gives us a chance to show that we are serious about having faith.

All those things that happened miraculously and immediately in Jesus' presence will happen to us *over time*, and in the normal course of affairs, in the afterlife. Some of our healing may happen here and now, but most of it will happen in the afterlife, where every tear will be dried, and all damage will be repaired. Healing is what Jesus does for us all the time, both here and in the afterlife, where we will have spiritual bodies. However, the healing is *usually* not instantaneous. What he did instantaneously for people when he was here in the flesh, he does with every one of us at the normal pace of growth and recovery. Jesus helps us with psychological healing. He heals people from shame and fear, makes them *whole*, and restores their self-respect—really, a greater miracle than any physical healing.

Although we rarely experience the *sudden* healing that occurred when Jesus was present in the flesh, we can plug into the same healing power. The gradualness of our healing may be a blessing, enabling us to observe and understand the working of God's creative influence on the spiritual and psychological levels.

Of course, here in this life we need to turn from purely physical living to spiritual living, to "the new life of the Spirit" (Rom 7:6). We must become spiritually reoriented, must be "born from above" (John 3:3), or "born again" (John 3:3 NIV). The physical life is the cocoon for the spiritual life. We cannot be saved if we never leave the cocoon, if we never break out of the eggshell. Salvation is rebirth, no longer living like an animal, but living like a child of God. Salvation means accepting new life, and a new *level* of life: "if anyone is in Christ, there is a new creation . . . everything has become new!" (2 Cor 5:17). We are to "be transformed by the renewing of your minds, so that you may discern what is the will of God" (Rom 12:2).

Spiritual growth is our purpose, our promise, our delight. The growth imperative is seen in the command "Be perfect, therefore, as your heavenly Father is perfect" (Matt 5:48), which is a statement about growth, not a demand for instantaneous perfection. We are *perfecting*, rather than *being* perfect. This is a goal for living. If we fail to see this, then it becomes an impossible standard that guarantees self-criticism and guilt, since we will always fall short. Falling short is to be expected, but we must be open to transformative change. Even if we suffer growing pains, we need to allow God to work on us. Seek God with all your heart: "you will find me; if you seek me with all your heart" (Jer 29:13). When we become partakers of the divine, the possibilities are limitless. But we will never reach a *final* perfection—thank God!

Maybe we can reach that place where "perfect love casts out fear" (1 John 4:18). Unfortunately, the persistence of religious fear and shame led to a distortion of the message of Jesus, and to a mythology about "the precious blood of Christ" (1 Pet 1:19). There is no magic in blood or violence, but there *is* salvation in the *person* of the Son: "'I am the resurrection and the life . . . Everyone who lives and believes in me will never die. Do you believe this?' She said to him, 'Yes, Lord, I believe'" (John 11:25–27). This woman is Martha, one of the underrated heroes of the faith: the first person in the Gospels to express faith in Jesus' resurrection power, his supremacy over death.

Jesus is and has always been the life-giver. He did not need to be murdered to be able to exercise that power.

BIBLIOGRAPHY

Abbott, Lyman. *The Evolution of Christianity*. Boston: Houghton Mifflin, 1893.

Allport, Gordon W., and Leo Postman. *The Psychology of Rumor*. New York: Russell & Russell, 1965.

Ansell, Nik. "Hell: The Nemesis of Hope?" Afterword in Bradley Jersak, *Her Gates Will Never Be Shut* , 191–210. Eugene, OR: Wipf & Stock, 2004.

Athanasius. *On the Incarnation of the Word*. Translated by a Religious of CSMV. Crestwood, NY: St. Vladimir's Seminary Press, 1988.

Bailey, Dan. "Biblical and Greco-Roman Uses of *Hilastērion* in Romans 3:25 and 4 Maccabees 17:22 (Codex S)." In Peter Stuhlmacher, *Biblical Theology of the New Testament,* translated and edited by Daniel P. Bailey, 824–68. Grand Rapids: Eerdmans, 2018.

Baker, Sharon L. *Executing God: Rethinking Everything You've Been Taught about Salvation and the Cross*. Louisville: Westminster John Knox, 2013.

———. *Razing Hell: Rethinking Everything You've Been Taught about God's Wrath and Judgment*. Louisville: Westminster John Knox, 2010.

Bartlett, Anthony W. *Cross Purposes: The Violent Grammar of Christian Atonement*. Harrisburg, PA: Trinity, 2001.

Bermann, Eric. *Scapegoat: The Impact of Death-Fear on an American Family*. Ann Arbor, MI: University of Michigan Press, 1973.

Bowne, Brendan Parker. *Studies in Christianity*. Boston: Houghton Mifflin, 1909.

Brock, Rita Nakashima, and Rebecca Ann Parker. *Proverbs of Ashes: Violence, Redemptive Suffering, and the Search for What Saves Us*. Boston: Beacon, 2001.

Bushnell, Horace. *The Vicarious Sacrifice Grounded in Principles of Universal Obligation*. New York: Scribner, 1868. (Orig. 1865.)

Calvin, Jean. *Institutes of the Christian Religion*. Translated by Henry Beveridge. Grand Rapids: Eerdmans, 1975.

Capps, Donald. *The Child's Song: The Religious Abuse of Children*. Louisville: Westminster John Knox, 1995.

Carroll, James. *Constantine's Sword: The Church and the Jews*. Boston: Houghton Mifflin, 2001.

Dawson, David. *Flesh Becomes Word: A Lexicography of the Scapegoat or, the History of an Idea.* East Lansing, MI: Michigan State University Press, 2013.

Drake-Brockman, Tom. *Bad Faith: A Spiritual Humanist Alternative for Christianity and the West.* Eugene, OR: Resource, 2019.

Dundes, Alan. "The Ritual Murder or Blood Libel Legend." In *The Blood Libel Legend: A Casebook in Anti-Semitic Folklore,* edited by Alan Dundes, 336–76. Madison, WI: University of Wisconsin Press, 1991.

Dunn, James D. G. *The Theology of Paul the Apostle.* Grand Rapids: Eerdmans, 1998.

Ehrman, Bart D. *The Orthodox Corruption of Scripture: The Effect of Early Christological Controversies on the Text of the New Testament.* Oxford: Oxford University Press, 1993.

Erikson, Erik H. *Young Man Luther: A Study in Psychoanalysis and History.* New York: Norton, 1962.

Evans, Rachel Held. *Inspired: Slaying Giants, Walking on Water, and Loving the Bible Again.* Nashville: Nelson, 2018.

Falk, Daniel R. *Coming to Peace with Science: Bridging the Worlds between Faith and Biology.* Downers Grove, IL: IVP Academic, 2004.

Finger, Thomas. "*Christus Victor* as Nonviolent Atonement." In *Atonement and Violence: A Theological Conversation,* edited by John Sanders, 87–111. Nashville: Abingdon, 2006.

Finlan, Stephen. *The Background and Content of Paul's Cultic Atonement Metaphors.* Academia Biblica 19. Atlanta: SBL/Brill, 2004.

———. *Problems with Atonement: The Origins of, and Controversy about, the Atonement Doctrine.* Collegeville, MN: Liturgical, 2005.

Finlan, Stephen, and Vladimir Kharlamov, eds. *Theōsis: Deification in Christian Theology.* Princeton Theological Monographs 52. Eugene, OR: Pickwick, 2006.

Forsyth, P. T. *The Person and Place of Jesus Christ.* Cincinnati: Jennings & Graham, 1909.

Frank, Doug. *A Gentler God: Breaking free of the Almighty in the Company of the Human Jesus.* Menangle, Australia: Albatross, 2010.

Goldstein, Phyllis. *A Convenient Hatred: The History of Antisemitism.* Brookline, MA: Facing History and Ourselves, 2012.

Graham, Billy. *Where I Am: Heaven, Eternity, and Our Life Beyond.* Nashville: W Publishing Group (Nelson), 2015.

Gregory of Nazianzen. "Epistle 101." In *Cyril of Jerusalem, Gregory of Nazianzen,* in the Nicene and Post-Nicene Fathers, Second Series [NPNF 2], volume 7, 439–443. Peabody, MA: Hendrickson, 2012. (Orig. 1894.)

Grensted, L. W. *A Short History of the Doctrine of the Atonement.* Manchester: Longmans, Green, 1920.

Grimsrud, Ted. *Instead of Atonement: The Bible's Salvation Story and Our Hope for Wholeness.* Eugene, OR: Cascade, 2013.

Holmes, Colin. "The Ritual Murder Accusation in Britain." In *The Blood Libel Legend: A Casebook in Anti-Semitic Folklore,* edited by Alan Dundes, 99–134. Madison, WI: University of Wisconsin Press, 1991.

Hsia, R. po-chia. *The Myth of Ritual Murder.* New Haven, CT: Yale University Press, 1988.

Hultgren, Arland J. *Paul's Gospel and Mission: The Outlook from His Letter to the Romans.* Philadelphia: Fortress, 1985.

Jersak, Bradley. *Her Gates Will Never Be Shut: Hell, Hope, and the New Jerusalem.* Eugene, OR: Wipf & Stock, 2004.

Kelly, J. N. D. *Early Christian Doctrines.* Rev. ed. New York: Harper & Row, 1978.

Lightfoot, J. B. *Saint Paul's Epistles to the Colossians and to Philemon.* Rev. ed. London: Macmillan, 1904.

Longenecker, Bruce W. *The Cross before Constantine: The Early Life of a Christian Symbol.* Minneapolis: Fortress, 2015.

Luther, Martin. *The Bondage of the Will.* In *Martin Luther: Selections from His Writings,* edited by John Dillenberger, 166–205. Garden City, NY: Doubleday, 1961.

McSorley, Harry J. *Luther: Right or Wrong? An Ecumenical-Theological Study of Luther's Major Work,* The Bondage of the Will. Minneapolis: Augsburg, 1969.

Miller, Alice. *For Your Own Good: Hidden Cruelty in Child-Rearing and the Roots of Violence.* Translated by Hildegarde and Hunter Hannum. New York: Farrar, Straus & Giroux, 1983.

Miller-McLemore, Bonnie J. *Let the Children Come: Reimagining Childhood from a Christian Perspective.* San Francisco: Jossey-Bass, 2003.

Ovesy, Lionel. "Introduction to Part I." In *Psychoanalysis: Toward the Second Century,* edited by Arnold M. Cooper, Otto F. Kernberg, and Ethel Spector Person, 9–11. New Haven, CT: Yale University Press, 1989.

Pattison, Stephen. "Shame and the Unwanted Self." In *The Shame Factor: How Shame Shapes Society,* edited by Robert Jewett, with Wayne L. Alloway Jr. and John G. Lacey, 9–29. Eugene, OR: Cascade, 2011.

Placher, William C. *Jesus the Savior: The Meaning of Jesus Christ for Christian Faith.* Louisville: Westminster John Knox, 2001.

Plato. *The Laws.* Translated by Trevor J. Saunders. Harmondsworth, UK: Penguin, 1975.

Rado, Sandor. "The Automatic Motivating System of Depressive Behavior." In *Psychoanalysis of Behavior; Collected Papers, vol. 2: 1956–1961,* 163–77. New York: Grune & Stratton, 1962.

———. "The Border Region between the Normal and the Abnormal: Four Types." In *Psychoanalysis of Behavior; Collected Papers, vol. 1: 1922–1956,* 324–31. New York: Grune & Stratton, 1956.

———. "The Problem of Melancholia." In *Psychoanalysis of Behavior; Collected Papers, vol. 1: 1922–1956,* 47–63. New York: Grune & Stratton, 1956.

————. "Rage, Violence, and Conscience." In *Psychoanalysis of Behavior; Collected Papers, vol. 2: 1956–1961,* 147–51. New York: Grune & Stratton, 1962.

Rappaport, Ernest A. "The Ritual Murder Accusation." In *The Blood Libel Legend: A Casebook in Anti-Semitic Folklore,* edited by Alan Dundes, 304–35. Madison, WI: University of Wisconsin Press, 1991.

Rashdall, Hastings. *The Idea of the Atonement in Christian Theology.* London: Macmillan, 1919.

Russell, Norman. *The Doctrine of Deification in the Greek Patristic Tradition.* Oxford: Oxford University Press, 2004.

Savary, Louis M. *Teilhard de Chardin*—The Divine Milieu *Explained: A Spirituality for the 21st Century.* Mahwah, NJ: Paulist, 2007.

Schultz, Magdalene. "The Blood Libel: A Motif in the History of Childhood." In *The Blood Libel Legend: A Casebook in Anti-Semitic Folklore,* edited by Alan Dundes, 273–303. Madison, WI: University of Wisconsin Press, 1991.

Segal, Alan F. *Life After Death: A History of the Afterlife in Western Religion.* New York: Doubleday, 2004.

Sklar, Jay. *Sin, Impurity, Sacrifice, Atonement: The Priestly Conceptions.* Hebrew Biblical Monographs 2. Sheffield: Sheffield Phoenix, 2005.

Thatcher, Adrian. *Theology and Families.* Challenges in Contemporary Theology. Oxford: Blackwell, 2007.

Thompson, Marianne Meye. *The Promise of the Father: Jesus and God in the New Testament.* Louisville: Westminster John Knox, 2000.

Wedderburn, Alexander J. M. *The Death of Jesus: Some Reflections on Jesus-Traditions and Paul.* WUNT 299. Tübingen: Mohr Siebeck, 2013.

Westcott, B. F., and F. J. A. Hort. *Introduction to the New Testament in the Original Greek with Notes on Selected Readings.* Peabody, MA: Hendrickson, 1988. (Orig. 1882.)

Wikipedia. "Blood Libel." https://en.wikipedia.org/wiki/Blood_libel.

Young, Frances M. *Construing the Cross: Type, Sign, Symbol, Word, Action.* Eugene, OR: Cascade, 2015.

————. *The Use of Sacrificial Ideas in Greek Christian Writers from the New Testament to John Chrysostom.* Eugene, OR: Wipf & Stock, 1979.

SUBJECT INDEX

NAME INDEX

ANCIENT DOCUMENTS INDEX